A Dictionary of

MILITARY
UNIFORM

A Dictionary of
MILITARY
UNIFORM

W. Y. Carman

Charles Scribner's Sons, New York

First published 1977
Copyright © W.Y. Carman 1977

1 3 5 7 9 11 13 15 17 19 I/C 20 18 16 14 12 10 8 6 4 2

Printed in Great Britain
Library of Congress Catalog Card Number 77-72064
ISBN 0-684-15130-8

Author's Note

It is hoped that readers will understand that this is a dictionary and therefore more limited than an encyclopaedia. It is intended to give those who consult this work the meaning of the word or subject but not every possible detail, which could take a heading into several pages or a book.

As frequently certain subjects may be known by different names, some slight duplication of information will be found (which would not be so in a history or chronological work) but each heading is meant to be self-explanatory. Obviously details of all badges, belt-plates and battle honours or even the many facing colours are not attempted in this dictionary, for an encyclopaedia or many volumes would be needed to cover such wide-ranging subjects.

Unless otherwise stated the description refers to the British Army although possibly it could apply to other nations. Although many attempts have been made to locate official documents to date certain items, it is to be noted that some more or less modern trade badges, etc. (not included in vocabularies or regulations) are vague as to dating. An official source states that such records are no longer kept. Thus if any reader or informed person can forward the writer such missing details, the information will be gratefully received.

Acknowledgments

The Author and Publishers would like to thank
L. Rousselot for Plates 1 and 2, and The Chief of Military
History and the Center of Military History, Washington
for Plates 10–13 and colour illustration 1. The National
Army Museum, London for the illustration on page 56
and Plates 19–21.
The remaining illustrations are from the Author's and
Publisher's collections.

Illustrations

Colour Illustrations

Ammunition Examiner. Embroidered arm badge

AD. Air Despatch. Embroidered arm badge

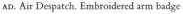

A This letter appears on arm badges in the British Army to indicate 'A' group of tradesmen, when the many tradesmen were divided into four groups in 1944 according to ACI 1236. Worn within sprays of laurel on the left forearm in old English style. White or buff embroidery on khaki for battledress (as also in other arm badges) and later embroidered in gold or silver wire for No. 1 Blues.

An 'A' embroidered in yellow on a black disk within red flames was introduced 30 November 1950 as the arm badge for an Ammunition Examiner (q.v.). Also made in brass.

Abzeichen German for insignia, the distinctions on uniform.

ACF These letters indicate the Army Cadet Force which was taken over by the War Office in April 1942. They wore the current battledress but now have jerseys. This means that many badges which were worn on the left arm must now be worn on the 'brassard' attached to the right shoulder button. This piece of fabric carries badges of rank, proficiency, titles, etc. See also Cert. A, Cert T. In 1974 the old certificate badges were replaced by new four-pointed stars of red or blue, bearing numbers from '1' to '4'. Another distinction of the ACF are the blue shoulder-strips worn by Adult and Cadet Under-Officers on their shoulder-straps.

See also Duke of Edinburgh's Awards and Rifles.

Achselbander German for shoulder-knot or aiguillette.

Achselklappen German for shoulder-strap.

Achselrolle German for small cloth roll on the shoulder to prevent strap or belt from slipping off.

Achelstucke German for shoulder-piece, usually denoting rank and/or unit.

Achseln Achsel wülste, German for 'wings', the cloth additions to the shoulders.

Accoutrements The personal equipment of a soldier other than arms or uniform, including belts, pouches, straps, packs, water-bottles and similar items.

Active Service and Peace Manoeuvres Forage Cap This long-titled ASPM cap is described in the 1883 Dress Regulations for infantry officers as the glengarry pattern worn by the men but not so high. In the Foot Guards the forage cap for active service and peace manoeuvres was a folding cap with side flaps worn by them as early as the Crimean War. It was similar to that worn in the Austrian army and is sometimes known as the Austrian cap. Variations of these caps were worn by other officers.

AD These letters on an arm badge denote 'Air Despatch' (q.v.). These letters and the surrounding circle were in yellow. A 'St Edward's Crown' (q.v.) was above in full colours and two light blue wings flanked the device, all being on a khaki ground.

ADC Abbreviation for aide-de-camp (q.v.). May be worn on an armlet.

Adler German for eagle, a device worn on helmets and buttons.

AE Ammunition Examiner (q.v.). The letters in a laurel wreath were worn on the arm by those qualified to examine live ammunition, which included dangerous explosives. Worn until about 1960.

Aeroplane spotter Better known as aircraft spotter (q.v.).

AFV These letters indicating Armoured Fighting Vehicles were worn with laurel as an arm badge for a short time after the First World War.

Aglet A small needle or point on a leather jerkin as worn under armour which served to affix the metal plates in position (see also aiguillette).

Agraffe An ornamental spray sometimes jewelled worn in front of oriental headdress.

Aide-de-camp Commonly given as ADC (q.v.). A staff officer who acts as aid to a senior officer, usually distinguished in modern times by an aiguillette. Early in the 19th century the ADC's coat was ornamented with special 'saw-edged' button-hole loops in gold or silver wire.

AIG Assistant Instructor in Gunnery, Royal Artillery. Wears an arm badge of crossed gun-barrels (q.v.) known in use before 1864.

Aigrette, egret Feather of heron, at base of hussar officers' plume.

Aiguillette A plaited cord ending with needles, points or aglets (q.v.) worn to distinguish several types of soldiers. (a) Staff, aiguillette No. 1, gold wire cord worn on the right, by Field-Marshals, ADC's to the Sovereign, equerries and other persons. Aiguillette No. 2, gold and crimson on the right for Military members of the Army Board personal staff of governors, etc. Aiguillette No. 3, gold and crimson but on the left shoulder for military attachés, various other ADC's, etc. There had been four grades but were reduced to three. Also once yeomanry and volunteer A.D.C.'s were permitted to wear silver aiguillettes instead of gold. (b) Household Cavalry. (i) all commissioned officers wear aiguillette on the right, on scarlet in the case of the Life Guards and on blue for the Royal Horse Guards, with stars of regimental pattern. (ii) 1st class staff aiguillette worn on left by WOI and II. (iii) 2nd class staff aiguillette worn by other NCOS on the left with no coils on end of cords. (iv) Simple aiguillette worn by lance corporals of Household Cavalry suspended from shoulder-strap, i.e. no shoulder-cords. (c) Bandsmen. By ACI 1135 of March 1925 bandsmen of dragoon guards and dragoons were allowed to wear aiguillettes on ceremonial parades at no expense to the public. (d) Aiguillettes had been worn much earlier by officers. In the 18th century the shoulder-knot was a plaited gold or silver cord with small needles but the development of the

ADC. Coat of an Aide-de-camp, *c.*1790

epaulette made the knot obsolete.

In the late 18th century the grades of general officers were given aiguillettes which served as a sign of rank although they did not yet carry stars or crowns. The heavy cavalry officers also had aiguillettes but they became obsolete in the reign of Queen Victoria. The newly-created lancers had aiguillettes also for a short time.

Air Battalion This branch of the Royal Engineers was in existence between 1911 and 1912 but had no special distinctions.

Aircraft spotter The badge of the aircraft spotter Class II is a blue bomber soaring upright. The Class I badge has the bomber within a blue embroidered wreath. They were introduced after World War Two and may be worn on No. 1 Dress in gold embroidery on blue ground.

Air Despatch Crews of RASC, later RCT, who qualify after certain drops or flights may wear an embroidered badge with 'AD' (q.v.).

Air Technician, REME Wears a trade badge, 'AT' within a crowned and winged circlet bearing REME, all yellow embroidered on blue.

Albert helmet Albert, the Prince Consort of Queen Victoria, being of German extraction had many ideas for progress in uniform. He replaced the 'Roman' helmet worn by heavy cavalry with a type based on the Prussian (or Russian) helmet then in wear. The Household Cavalry took their new pattern into wear in 1842 and the cavalry of the line about 1847. With minor alterations the helmets continued until the last days of full dress of cavalry and until today by the Household Cavalry.

Albert Shako, Chaco After more than one essay, the shako evolved by the Prince Consort for British infantry was a tubular affair with front and back peaks. This was in wear from 1844 until 1855 not only by the infantry but also the Royal Artillery and the Royal Engineers.

Alkalak, alkhalak Long coat worn by Indian cavalrymen, fastening on the chest.

Alligator This creature was a badge worn by the 19th Light Dragoons at the end of the 18th century. The regiment was raised in Jamaica where the alligator formed the crest of the Jamaican coat-of-arms. It also appeared on belt-plates and buttons of other Jamaican units.

Amalgamation The many reductions of units of the British Army result in efforts to keep in being many famous regiments which would otherwise disappear. Thus amalgamations of two regiments see the elements of both being continued as in the case of the red coat of the Scots Greys with the yellow facings of the 3rd Dragoon Guards (Carabiniers) when they became the Royal Scots Dragoon Guards in 1971. Titles worn on the shoulders also indicate former units as in the case of the 4/7 Dragoon Guards and the 16/5 Lancers. But infantry regiments frequently take new titles

Albert helmet. Officer 6th Dragoon Guards, *c.*1850

Albert shako. Officer, 1st Bombay Native Infantry, c.1850

and distinctions so that the former regiments are not obvious.

Ammunition boots Many articles from public stores which were issued to soldiers received the prefix of 'ammunition', such as 'ammunition loaf', with the idea of indicating the source of issue.

Ammunition examiner This tradesman or trained soldier wore at first the arm badge with AE and laurels (q.v.) which changed about 1950 to the elaborate 'A' with flames (q.v.).

Andrews' hat Colonel T P Andrews who commanded the newly raised regiment of Voltigeurs and Foot Rifles in the American Army of 1847 requested a new type of hat for his men. This was soft felt with a wide brim which could be worn down in wet weather or strong sun but was also capable of folding flat. Although approved they were not issued until 1851 and served to be the forerunner of the campaign hat of 1872. Also known as the Voltigeur hat (q.v.).

Angreke, angreeka Type of loose jacket worn by Indian infantry in the 18th century.

Ankle boots Shoes were worn in the British Army until 1823 when half-boots were to be worn. Boots were issued without eyelet holes, the idea being that the wearer pierced the holes best suited to his feet. Boots were not made left and right but were expected to be worn on alternate feet to give even wear on the soles. Separate lasts were introduced in 1838. The laced boot was replaced by the 'cossack' boot in 1838. Ankle boots came back in 1873. Light patterns for walking out were approved in 1925. 'Boots, ankle, DMS' (directly moulded soles) were issued in 1963.

Boots which had been blackened were left uncoloured in time of war, dubbing being used in the First World War to preserve them. Officers boots were polished brown in 1902 but other ranks remained black.

Anklets Made of web canvas with two straps and brass buckles were worn experimentally in 1932. They were finally approved for wear in 1938 when battle dress was issued to other ranks. Sometimes worn in tropical climates with hosetops instead of short puttees. All-leather anklets were later introduced, being popular with the Home Guard.

APJI Assistant Parachute Jumping Instructor. The yellow initials APJI were embroidered under a white parachute and

APJI. Embroidered arm badge of Assistant Parachute Jumping Instructor

surrounded by a green wreath. Light blue wings were on either side of this badge. This appointment was originally given the normal parachute badge in 1942 but in 1955 had the badge described above.

Appointments Apart from meaning posts to which a person might be appointed, the word also relates to 'places of distinction' in a military unit. The warrant of 1768 stated that 'no colonel is to put his Arms, Device or Livery, on any part of the Appointments of the Regiment under his command'. This would cover standards and regimental colours, drums, officers' gorgets and cross-belt plates. When battle honours or special regimental distinctions were granted these would be placed on the appointments. In the case of rifle regiments the plate on the shoulder belt frequently carried the many honours.

Apprentice Young soldiers are frequently trained at apprentice schools and colleges. They may wear a special badge or may also have the companies or wings distinguished by differently coloured markings on the arm or shoulder-strap.

Apron (a) The pioneer of infantry or the farrier of cavalry from the 18th century onward frequently had dirty manual tasks to perform and needed a leather apron to protect his uniform. The apron worn today is more ceremonial than practical, although the dismounted farrier still has shoeing to undertake. (b) The introduction of the bass drum to dismounted bandsmen brought the need of protection for the chest of the coat. At the beginning of the 19th century the leather or material apron which reached to the knees was sufficient, but the availability of animal skins (mainly from India) brought about the use of leopard and tiger skins, in most cases with the claws and complete head hanging down the back of the drummer. (c) As the swinging side drum caused friction on the left leg, knee aprons were frequently worn with either three or two straps fastened behind the leg. (d) Heavy wind instruments also caused wear on tunic. Household Brigade bands may be seen wearing the apron, often of scarlet cloth. Rifle regiments wear black leather or cloth protectors.

Arm bands In the English Civil War, bands or strips of white cloth might be worn around the upper arm to denote the field mark of the day, made necessary at a time when opposing troops wore similar dress.

Later, in Napoleonic times, some foreign troops attached to the British Army wore arm bands on their own uniforms, presumably to avoid accidental shooting.

Arm Blanche This French expression referred to the 'white arms' as opposed to firearms, thus mainly indicating cavalry armed with swords or lances, i.e. in white metal.

Armel aufschlag German. Cuff or turn-up to sleeves.

Armel patten German. The small patch or flap on the cuffs.

Armlet Officers and men carrying out special duties of a temporary nature and with need of quick recognition wear armlets or

15

Arm of service stripe. Three red stripes indicating 160th Brigade of 53rd Welsh Division

Army Recruiter. Embroidered arm badge of time of Queen Elizabeth II

brassards (q.v.), usually with letters to indicate their work. EMBARK and RTO (Railway transport officer) are typical needs in the time of war, while MP or RMP are quickly recognised in peacetime. In wartime the many staff duties are indicated on red and blue armlets. In the First World War certain officers wore the divisional sign on a red armlet and the new blue and white armlet was well-known for the Signal Corps. There are many varieties, some of which are obsolete but others which remain in use with slight changes.

Arm of Service strip In May 1940 a system of identifying the arms of service in battle dress was being considered. The German army had its *waffenfarbe* by which a branch of the army could be easily distinguished. In September 1940 an ACI was issued by which officers had coloured underlay to the rank badge and the men narrow strips of cloth (2 ins by $\frac{1}{4}$ in) on the upper arm. By the end of the war the following distinctions had been worn – Staff, red; Royal Armoured Corps, yellow and red; Reconnaisance Corps, green and yellow; Royal Artillery, red and blue; Royal Engineers, blue and red; Royal Corps of Signals, blue and white; infantry, scarlet; rifle regts, green; Royal Army Chaplain Department, black (later purple); RASC, yellow and blue; RAMC, dull cherry; RAOC, blue (later red blue red); REME, red yellow and blue; CMP, red; Royal Army Pay Corps, yellow (later yellow blue yellow); Royal Army Educational Corps, Cambridge blue; Royal Army Dental Corps, green and white; Army Air Corps, light blue and dark blue; Royal Pioneer Corps, red and green; Intelligence Corps, green; Army Physical Training Corps, black red black; Army Catering Corps, grey and yellow. Officers wore the first-mentioned colour under their badges and the men's shoulder-strips were worn with the first colour foremost. Further distinctions within a division included arm of service strips being worn in one, two or three rows to indicate senior, intermediate and junior brigade but variations took place.

Armour Although it might seem that armour belongs to the Middle Ages rather than the period of uniform, the helmet, cuirass and gorget continued into the 19th and 20th centuries (see under cuirass, gorget and helmet).

Armoured car Badge of a unit so equipped. As all members of a 'tank' unit wore the badge of a tank on the upper right arm, the precedent seemed made for men of an armoured car unit to follow in their own fashion. The 12th Royal Lancers wore the badge on their sleeve which was a regimental tradesmen's badge, equivalent to Class B and denoted a fully trained a/c crewsman.

Army Cadet Force See under ACF for distinctions, also Cert. A and T.

Army Recruiter Originally regiments recruited their own men but after the 1914–18 war the Paid Pensioner Recruiter who carried out this work was given a blue uniform (full dress had been discontinued for other ranks) and this bore badges with PPR. In

1933 the title became Army Recruiter and that title was to be on the shoulders with 'GR' in the cap badge. Later these men were allowed to wear on the upper arm the embroidered badge of two crossed Union Colours (the crossed flags for colour-sergeants had disappeared just before the First World War). After the Second World War, the Women's Royal Army Corps wearing their own uniform plus the Army Recruiting distinction undertook such duties at the Central London Recruiting Depot.

Artificer This title for a craftsman covers many trades. The term was in use in the mid-19th century when the wheeler (who made wheels) and the carpenter wore the arm badge of a wheel (q.v.). Ordnance artificers wore badges of the hammer and pincers as well as the wheel. In 1944 the A, B, C and D groups of tradesmen replaced the hammer and pincers badge except in the artillery.

Artillery A branch of the Army but originally under the Board of Ordnance. At first wore the red coat with blue cuffs as other soldiers in Charles II's reign but in the reign of George I the dark blue coat with red facings was adopted as a more practical garment. The grenade (or flaming bomb) is a badge for the artillery as is the gun (q.v.). For trade badges see under AIG, G, L, HO, etc. The Foot Artillery wore a version of the infantry uniform whereas the Horse Artillery was based on the Hussar with whom they were to act in combat.

Assault Pioneer This modern category of infantryman wears the badge of crossed axes (q.v.) which have long been the sign of an ordinary pioneer.

Astrakhan, astrachan This tightly curled black fur, normally lambskin, was used for trimming British officers' frock-coats. The fur caps worn during the Canadian winters were occasionally made of astrakhan fur.

AT These initials appear within the usual sprays to indicate an anti-tank gun-layer. Worn after the Second World War it appears on the left forearm as a badge of skill, although it has been seen above chevrons on the right arm.

AT In the centre of the Air Technician (REME) badge (q.v.).

Atholl grey The particular shade of grey worn by Foot Guards officers for the greatcoat and cape and noted as such back in Edwardian times.

Athwart The contemporary term for the fashion of wearing the cocked hat of two peaks with the corners over the shoulders. If worn with the peaks to the front and rear, it was called 'fore-and-aft', both terms being naval in use in Napoleonic times for both army and navy headdress. When the new fashion of the peak in front appeared, many old-fashioned officers continued for years to wear the bicorn 'athwart'.

Attila German. A type of single-breasted tunic worn by hussars from the mid-19th century onwards.

Austrian Cap In the middle of the 19th century an undress cap sometimes called the Austrian Cap was popular. This folded flap

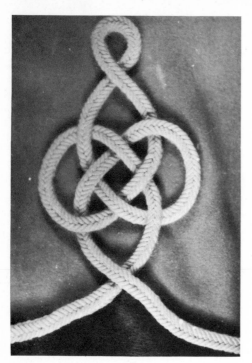

Austrian knot. Cuff of full dress tunic, sapper of Royal Engineers

with two large side flaps which could be turned down or up and was practical in bad weather. Although worn extensively by the Austrian soldiers the British Foot Guards had a similar cap in the Crimean War. In 1880 it was 'generally introduced' as an active service and peace manoeuvres cap, sometimes nicknamed the 'tea-cosy'. The term also applied to a later pattern.

Austrian knot This special knot was worn in braid on the sleeves of tunics, not only of Austrian troops but in the late 19th century by the British Army.

Austrian wave This pattern of gold or silver lace was a special distinction for the Austrian army from the late 18th century onwards. It was adopted by the British 15th Hussars in the early 19th century and has been worn by other cavalry regiments also.

Axes Badge of pioneers (q.v.). Crossed axes (also called hatchets) were and are worn on the upper arm. Worn by French pioneers in the 18th century but not adopted by the British until the next. Also worn with various regimental badges above.

Backing. Rank badge of major on red background

Backing. Eagle of Royal Dragoons on black ground

B Appears within laurel wreath as badge of 'B' group tradesmen (see also 'A' for further information).

Backing (a) Headdress badges frequently have backings of black or coloured cloth to enhance the visibility. The centre of helmet badges introduced *c.*1880 sometimes had black velvet (or red). Unofficially in time of war were mounted on colour patches but this practice was frowned upon. Red was used by royal regiments, green or black by rifle or light infantry regiments but almost any colour might have appeared. (b) Rank badges. In May 1940 a scheme was being considered to place officers embroidered badges of rank on patches of colour to indicate branch of service. This was eventually carried out not only on battle dress but in service dress and in tropical dress (q.v. arm of service for colours).

Badges There are many categories of badges in use in the British Army serving a variety of purposes but mainly of identification. Badges had been in use in the Middle Ages when they were employed to distinguish noble families as part of heraldic art. Some of the groups are as follows. (a) Badges on uniform would seem to have been first on the headdress. The early grenadier caps with an embroidered front were good vehicles for the Sovereign's or the colonel's cypher or coat-of-arms. Early metal badges are those like the portcullis which appears on caps of Honorable Artillery Company in George I's reign. The introduction of light cavalry and light infantry in the mid-18th century saw metal badges in use. When hats gave place to shakos, plates which were in fact large badges were worn. Plates continued on the infantry helmet and of course the cavalry headdresses.

Apart from full-dress headdress, badges were worn on undress caps. The soft caps of the early 19th century were not suitable for badges although large embroidered initials are known. The stiff forage cap of Prussian origin allowed devices and badges to be worn, either embroidered or of metal. Officers might wear regimental badges but other ranks at first were only allowed metal numerals, with the possible addition of a crown for royal regiments, a grenade for fusiliers or grenadier companies, or a bugle horn for light infantry or light companies. The introduction of glengarry caps for all infantry *c.*1870 saw the production of special regimental badges which continued to develop on following undress and service caps.

(b) Belt-plates, pouches and other items of equipment were also places for badges. Uniform collars and shoulder-straps in the 19th century might also have badges and mounted badges appeared on buttons. Collar badges for other ranks were introduced *c.*1872 following an attempt at economy in 1871 when a common general

Badge. Metal badges on cap of grenadier officer, Honourable Artillery Company, time of George I

Badges of Rank. In metal for general officer, major and 2nd lieutenant

service button replaced many of the regimental patterns of infantry other ranks. Cavalry regiments did not acquire collar badges until many years later. NCOs of most cavalry regiments wore a special regimental badge over their chevrons or badge of rank. In the early 19th century a crown of the Prince of Wales' feathers was to be seen but by the end of the century most cavalry regiments had their own pattern as did many yeomanry regiments. The Royal Artillery NCOs had their gun badge, the Royal Engineers the grenade, the Royal Signals the figure of Mercury, and so on. Infantry of the line did not have special arm badges although an 'eagle' for the Essex Regiment is known.

(c) Rank badges began to develop in the 19th century and may be referred to under that heading. It was not until the first decade that infantry officers had their own system and some cavalry officers reached the middle of the century without rank badges. Badges of rank for NCOs which were chevrons were approved in 1802 and they were augmented during the following years, that for the colour sergeant appearing on 5 July 1813. In the American Army officers' badges of rank included stars, bars, eagles and oakleaves.

(d) There were badges of appointment given to trumpeters, drummers, buglers and pipers. Senior NCOs in the Royal Artillery, Royal Engineers and Royal Signals had their own badges added to the rank badges. The musicians mentioned above were without badges for many years. The drummer of the 18th century had the badge of a drum on his cap and it was not until the 19th century that he wore it on his sleeve. Buglers and trumpeters had arm badges in the 19th century but it was not until 1949 that badges were approved for Scottish and Irish pipers (see also under separate titles).

(e) In the 19th century there were many soldiers who qualified for skill-at-arms badges. Many categories began as awards or prize badges for swordsmanship, lance drill, gunnery, driving and musketry. The First World War saw the abolition of prizes but peace brought back many of the competition badges as skill-at-arms awards. The wider coverage includes some which might have been considered trade or appointment. The trade of farrier goes back to the 18th century and the horseshoe was worn as a trade sign, at first in the front of his fur cap but later on the arm. There are many other trade badges to be noted throughout this work. There were also qualified instructors (also dealt with elsewhere) who included a special badge with their rank marking. The spur for riding also featured for the riding instructor, the crossed swords for proficiency in that weapon also was worn by instructors in physical training and the Assistant Parachute Jumping Instructor of modern days has his own extra badge (q.v.).

Bag This normally applied to the cloth appendage of the fur cap or busby and was originally the cap before the fur was added. As the fur edge increased in size throughout the years the cap gradually disappeared until only a tip appeared through the top, falling where it may. The bag is now a piece of flattened cloth attached to a circular piece which can be removed from the busby when needed. Originally British hussars had red bags, the 18th being an exception with light blue, but other colours were introduced later. In the last days of full dress the colours were as follows – garter blue for 3rd Hussars, yellow for 4th, scarlet for 7th, 8th, 10th and 15th, crimson for 11th and 20th, buff for 13th, crimson for 18th, white for 19th and French grey for 21st. These are for other ranks; variations took place for officers when amalgamations occurred in 1922.

Bagpipe The badge of a bagpipe is worn on the right arm to signify a person qualified to play either the Scottish or the Irish pipes, the latter badge having one drone less. It was not until 16 March 1949 that the use of these badges was generally approved although pipers had been noted in the army as early as the 17th century.

Balaclava The name of this famous Crimean battle is applied to a type of knitted cap, no doubt made at that time. The balaclava, which is like a close-fitting hood over the head and neck but open in the face, was very popular in the First World War. It was usually of knitted khaki wool.

Baldrick, baldric Is a belt which hung from the right shoulder to the left hip, normally holding a sword, but a drum could also be carried. They were worn until the 18th century and were often, in the case of officers, embroidered and stitched.

Ball-buttons These round buttons were worn on the clothing of hussars, riflemen and horse artillery and various yeomanry regiments. Normally the round ball is of metal, gilt or brass for horse artillery, silver or gilt for cavalry and silver or black composition for rifle regiments. Early light cavalry wore jackets with ball buttons in the centre row but with half-balls on the outer rows. Buttons may be plain or with an inscription.

Bagpipe. Metal arm badge for Scottish piper

Infantry bandsmen, c. 1890

Band badge. Arm badge embroidered on khaki, early 20th century

Balloon School, Royal Engineers Although this 'flying' branch was in being until 1911 before the Royal Flying Corps was formed it had no special uniform. See also Air Battalion.

Ball Tuft A ball of wool or cotton worn in front of a shako from about 1829 onwards. In the case of the rifles the ball was black. In 1830 light companies and light infantry had green ball tufts. In 1835 the tuft was white for all line regiments and fusiliers. In 1846 the line regiments had white and red ball tufts and much later Royal regiments had all red. The 34th Foot has a special privilege of red over white and the 46th had permission for red much earlier.

Balmoral A Scottish bonnet but also made in England in the First World War when drab instead of blue issues were made.

Band The band of music introduced into regiments and corps in the 18th century was not expected to be part of the fighting force, unlike the drummers and buglers. They wore a special dress which was paid for by the colonel or by the officers from a band fund. As the musicians in the early days were often foreigners, including many Germans, they may have brought continental fashions, for the dress was often colourful and elaborate. It became the fashion for infantry bands to wear white clothing and in 1830 they were officially ordered to wear white with regimental facings. In 1834 heavy cavalry bands were ordered to wear scarlet coats. The Household Cavalry and the Foot Guards being troops of the Sovereign had special state clothing heavily laced with gold – a costume which dated from the late 17th century. In 1871 infantry bands had begun to wear red tunics similar to the ordinary soldier but distinguished by the musician's wings on the shoulders. Rifle regiments of course wore green with red and black braid for the King's Royal Rifle Corps and black for the Rifle Brigade. After the First World War permission was granted for officers to return to full dress for levees and similar occasions. Permission was not granted to other ranks (except in the case of Household troops) but as bands were considered an aid to recruiting permission for full dress with peaked caps was granted. After the Second World War the re-introduction of full dress for bands was delayed until the 1950s. Scottish bands managed to find many occasions when full dress including feather bonnets might be worn and tattoos now have many colourful bands.

Band badge Although a special band badge or plate may have been worn on shakos it was not until the introduction of the red tunic for infantry bandsmen that a new arm badge was introduced. Crossed trumpets combined with a harp were worn by some but the Grecian lyre became the popular distinction, still worn today usually combined with oakleaves and a crown. It is worn on the right arm in both ceremonial and service dress.

Bandelier German for pouch belt.

Bandmaster As the early military bands were employed civilians so were early bandmasters. These men did not always accompany the band on marches and were not deemed the equivalent of officers. The uniform of the bandmaster was more elaborate than that of the bandsmen but it was not until the end of the 19th century that they wore the undress uniform of an officer but without rank markings. By the turn of the century the band-master was beginning to receive commissioned rank and thus also officers' clothing with the band badge on the lower right arm. After the First World War long frock coats were popular among bandmasters and are still worn today, in the case of cavalry regi-ments with waistbelts and swords.

Bandolier This is equipment rather than uniform but it is part of the soldier's dress. The early 'bandaleer' (from the Spanish *banda*, a sash) referred to the belt which held powder cases in the 17th century. These small containers (wood or leather) each con-tained enough gunpowder for one loading of a musket. As 12 cases were often carried on a belt by means of strings the bandolier was given the nickname of the 'Twelve Apostles'. They become obsolete at the end of the 17th century.

The 19th century colonial wars brought the need for the mounted rifleman to have a readily accessible supply of cartridges. Thus in the late 19th century a belt was worn over the left shoulder which had loops for either separate cartridges or pouches for ammunition in clips. The passing of the horse after the First World War saw the obsolescence of the bandolier.

Bar (a) May refer to the ornamental bars on the back of a hussar's jacket. (b) Bars are also worn by medical orderlies. One bar of tubular braid, cherry-coloured, worn on the cuff marks the 2nd class orderly, RAMC. Two bars indicate a 1st class orderly. The same system marks the orderlies in the Royal Army Dental Corps but the colour is emerald green.

Barathea A material used by officers for the service dress uniform – a fine woollen cloth which can be made with or without silk or cotton. Popular in the First World War.

Barenfell German, bearskin, used as horse furnishing.

Barett German, beret.

Barrel (a) A girdle or sash of hussars has small cylindrical tubes to keep the long cords in place and these are called barrels, originally worn loose but later fixed in groups.

(b) Ornaments on the back of the early hussars jackets.

Bars In the American Army bars were used to distinguish some officers, one silver for a 1st lieutenant, two silver for a captain and at first none for the 2nd lieutenant, although he was later given a gold bar. In the Confederate Army, captains had three bars, 1st lieutenant two and a 2nd lieutenant one bar.

Bass-drummer The large drum carried in military bands by the bass-drummer could damage the uniform, thus a large protective apron covering the chest and waist was worn (q.v. apron). This drummer's uniform was occasionally more elaborate than the drummers.

Bath Star. On officer's belt-plate of 57th Middlesex Regiment, c.1852

Battle honour. Cap badge of Border Regiment with 13 named battles.

Bath Star The Order of the Bath which was granted to many military leaders had a distinctive star. This was frequently borne on the breastplate of officers and is the pattern for the star rank badge of officers.

Baton The baton or staff of Greek and Roman times was originally a simple piece of wood, useful for indication or, it is said, for secret messages with the paper wound round the staff. Although the baton evolved on the Continent British generals had to be content with a wooden staff until the Prince Regent congratulated the Duke of Wellington after a victory as having 'won his baton'. When the Duke pointed out that there was no baton, one was specially made for him and they became available for other officers. The rank badge of general officers includes a baton crossed over a sword and field marshals have two crossed batons as a badge.

Battalion company The basic companies in a regiment were known as the battalion companies. The extra flank companies were the grenadier and the light companies. The battalion companies in the 18th century wore the common hat and were also called the 'hat-companies' which term ceased when shakos came in use.

Battle dress Although this term could apply to any uniform worn in battle, in Great Britain it refers to the special garments developed before the Second World War. In March 1938 a trial uniform likened to that worn for ski-ing was demonstrated. A blouse, ski-type trousers and webbing gaiters were among the items later adopted and worn in the next conflict. Other ranks in 1944 were given a collared shirt and tie thus allowing the blouse to be worn open. In 1961 the battle dress became obsolescent.

Battle honours Officers, and to a lesser extent other ranks, were given personal medals when they took part in a successful battle in the 18th century. The idea of special battle honours for a regiment or unit slowly evolved. The 15th Light Dragoons, were so successful at the Battle of Emsdorf in July 1760, that they noted that name on their headdress. The long siege of Gibraltar from 1779 to 1783 was also permitted to be marked on the head-dress of grenadiers of those regiments present. Perhaps it was the presence of Hanoverian troops that encouraged such a departure. Hanoverian infantry regiments wore a cuff band with 'Gibraltar' until the present century. The campaigns against Napoleon brought new battle honours to the British army – the 'Sphinx for Egypt' being a striking distinction which still appears in many cap badges. Battle honours were permitted to be worn on appointments, which included shako and belt-plates of officers as well as regimental colours and drums. They may also appear on cap badges and buttons.

Baudrier French for baldrick or shoulder-belt.

Bayonet Apart from being a side-arm, the bayonet is also part of an arm badge (with a wreath) for proficiency in the cadet force.

Bayonet belt In the early 18th century the common soldier had a waistbelt which carried both his sword and his bayonet. By the middle of the century the sword for an infantryman was obsolescent and the fashion of wearing the bayonet belt over the shoulder saw the introduction of belt plates for infantrymen. Although not as elaborate as those for officers, these plates often assumed a regimental device as well as the precedence number. In the 19th century the bayonet reverted to a waistbelt but with a separate frog for suspension.

Bay A type of reddish-brown horse. As the 2nd Dragoon Guards were mounted on horses of this colour, they were called the 'Bays'. It is a coincidence that the regimental badge included a laurel-wreath, the leaves of which are also known as 'bay'.

Beading This refers to the fine metalwork beads which appear on epaulettes and some belt-plates.

Beard Although the wearing of a beard might have been popular in the Royal Navy it was not encouraged in the British Army. However, after campaigns like that of the Crimea when beards had to be worn because of the bad weather, they were permitted for a certain period when the troops returned home, thus allowing recognition of veterans. With the advent of volunteer soldiers and the Home Guards of recent years, a civilian could retain his beard.

Officially tolerated were the beards of pioneers and pipers. In the case of pioneers they were expected to lead the troops into action and clear the way and so the beard has been worn by some regimental pioneers in modern times. The reason for pipers is not as ancient or as explicable.

Bearskin The fur caps worn by Foot Guards are known as 'bearskins'. Caps worn by grenadiers in the 17th century could be either of cloth or made with fur. Fur caps were authorised to all grenadiers in 1768. When the 1st Foot Guards were named Grenadiers after Waterloo (and the other foot guards later received similar distinctions) all men wore the fur cap or bearskin. Recent rises in the cost of bearskins led to experiments with nylon fur but the aid of the Canadians restored the original fur.

Beaver This name was applied to hats in the 17th century. It is possible that many civilian hats were not made from the genuine beaver animal but that 'coney' (rabbit) was made to simulate beaver.

Bedford cord A strong cloth with ribbed or corded surface originally developed in Bedford, USA, was popular at the end of the 19th century for cavalry breeches.

Beinkleider German for trousers.

Bekleidung German for clothing.

Bell crown cap The 'bell crown' of American headdress is mentioned in the 1821 uniform regulations and was worn until 1832. The concave sides led up to a wide top following the European style.

Belt There are many types of belt in the British Army ranging from the practical to the ornamental. Originally the belt or strap

Bearskin. Fur cap of officer of the Foot Guards, period of William IV.

Belt Plate. Officer of 49th Foot, c.1820-42

Bicorn. Heavy Cavalry officer, c.1812

Bisley badge. Embroidered arm badge for Bisley competitions

should have a buckle or fastening but not always as in the case of the colour-belt which is sewn and more correctly known as a sash or scarf. See also waistbelt, shoulder-belt, pouch-belt and sword-belt.

Belted plaid Before the introduction of the little kilt, the upper garment of a Highlander was the plaid (breccan). This large piece of tartan was pleated and belted around the waist so that the lower part formed the kilt and the upper part either protected the body or was folded at the back and fastened at the shoulder. In the early years of the Black Watch they wore the belted plaid.

Belt plate This metal item although thought by some to be an ornament was originally the fastening which replaced the buckle on belts. It became common in the last part of the 18th century for officers' sword belts and other ranks' bayonet belts when they were worn over the shoulder. Hence it is some times called the shoulder belt plate or the cross belt plate. The first plate on the shoulder belt (which was the old waist belt) had been of a horizontal design. When in the shoulder position the plate 'read' sideways and new patterns had to be designed which were upright. Engraved plates gave way to cast plates and later polished back plates had elaborate mounts fastened to them, although the soldiers' plate was much plainer. The Crimean War saw the end of such plates except in the case of Scottish regiments which continued to wear the shoulder belt for the Scottish broadsword to modern times.

Beret Although the Tank Corps had its origin in the First World War it was not until 1924 that the black beret was approved for wear. This practical headdress for wear inside a tank was inspired by the Basque beret worn by the French troops. The French Chasseurs d'Alpine had worn the beret in the 19th century and Spanish troops had worn it even earlier. The 11th Hussar when made an armoured car unit were in 1932 permitted a ginger-brown or 'crushed strawberry' beret with a crimson head-band. When the Royal Dragoons were mechanised in the Second World War their commanding officer chose a grey beret but this was discontinued at the end of the war. In 1943 both the commandos and the airborne forces were permitted coloured berets, the former green and the latter maroon. What was called a khaki beret but was actually a cap, g.s. (general service) was issued to Irish troops in 1943. In 1950 blue berets were issued for wear with battle dress, rifle regiments (and later light infantry) wore green and the Army Air Corps had light blue. Various embellishments like hackles and coloured patches were worn as well as badges. When troops of the United Nations went on peace-keeping missions, all nationalities wore the light blue beret.

BG The arm badge of a bren-gunner bears these initials within a laurel wreath either in khaki or in colour.

Bicorn, bicorne A hat with two corners or peaks. Originally worn with the points over the shoulders, then pointing front and rear. Today in the British Army, called the cocked hat.

Black musician. A – 3rd Regiment of Foot Guards; B – Grenadier Guards

Binde German for band. A white band or cloth was worn on the left upper arm by Prussian and Austrian troops in 1814 and 1864.

Binocular case At the end of the 19th century officers of general staff, Royal Artillery and Royal Engineers carried small binoculars in a case in the middle of the back.

Bisley badge An embroidered badge with crossed muskets and the word 'BISLEY' signifies musketry success in the Cadet Hundred competition at Bisley.

Bit The embroidered badge of a bit was the trade badge worn by the saddler and collar maker of cavalry in the last half of the 19th century and is still worn on the right upper arm.

Black-cock feathers These black and white feathers were worn on the full dress of the Royal Scots and the King's Own Scottish Borderers, also by pipers with glengarries. Black cock's feathers were also used for the plume in the cocked hats of surgeons in the 19th century.

Black line in lace Some regiments have the tradition that the black line in their lace is a sign of mourning for a famous person or soldier (see also mourning). But such a tradition is often difficult to substantiate. The black line could appear either in the officers' metal lace or the men's worsted braid. Before 1830 many regular regiments had silver lace and the black line was added to heighten the pattern. Not all black lines were continued after 1830 when regulars were to wear gold only. In the 1883 Dress Regulations after the re-organisation of infantry eight regiments had black lines in the officers' lace (two at least for the first time although the other ranks' braid had black lines many years earlier.

Black musicians 'Black-a-moors' were frequently employed in military bands, no doubt because they were thought 'exotic' and brought a new sense of rhythm. At the end of the 18th century Foot Guards' bands had special time-beater groups, which might include drum, cymbals and tambourine. The 4th Dragoons are known to have had six black musicians as early as 1715. It was usual to give these men fanciful clothing like turbans and Oriental (or Turkish) dress but by the reign of Queen Victoria they were used very little.

Bladder A bladder was worn between the hat and the lining for regiments proceeding to the West Indies in 1761, no doubt so as to limit the heat.

Blanco This preparation introduced c.1835 replaced whiting as a substance to clean and preserve equipment. Many variations of colouring were found necessary in the First World War and even draughtsmen's white ink was known to replace it.

Blanket coat (see also Maud) In the 18th century overcoats were not issued to all infantrymen although a certain number of 'watch-coats' were available for the sentries on duty at night. Blankets were frequently worn in the American winters and even in the Mediterranean area.

Blanket pin This very large and strong version of a safety pin

27

was used to fasten the fly of the Highland kilt.

Blouse This loose garment was worn in the early 20th century by mounted troops in India. It was also popular at the time of Garibaldi, when red was a favourite colour. In modern time the thick upper garment of the battle dress was known as the blouse.

Blücher boot This is a handsewn leather boot worn by the British soldiers until 1913 when it was replaced by the Army ankle boot.

Blue clothing Although the red coat had been the mark of the British soldier since the 16th century, blue coats were also worn by Royalist troops, no doubt because the colour was a royal one. The Royal Horse Guards had been the 'Oxford Blues' even before they became Royal cavalry at the time of the Restoration. The 10th Foot raised by the Earl of Bath in 1685 wore blue coats for several years. When William of Orange, later William III, came to England his troops had blue coats and it was popular for new English regiments to appear in the blue coat also. But by the time of Queen Anne the red coat was the normal wear. George I brought the blue coat for the artillery and it was not until late in the 18th century that blue clothing was to be worn by light dragoons. Light cavalry including hussars and lancers kept the colour (except for a few years of William IV's reign) up to the last days of full dress. Many corps created in the last part of the 19th century also wore blue tunics.

For undress, infantry officers wore blue frocks, keeping scarlet for full dress. When the First World War saw the discontinuance of full dress for other ranks, khaki was the only dress available. The Coronation of 1936 saw blue uniforms being issued in limited quantities. After the Second World War when again a smarter uniform was thought necessary, the 'No. 1 Blues' were introduced (Scottish regiments being permitted 'piper green' and of course Rifle regiments had their own shade of green).

Bomb The badge of a bomb was chosen to indicate the Bomb Disposal units of the Second World War. The yellow bomb on a scarlet oval was worn on the forearm by regular troops. The bomb disposal units of the Home Guard had their own version with two crossed bombs. (See also 'AE'.)

Bombay bloomers These long and large pants were manufactured in Bombay and had tapes threaded through the leg bottoms which could be turned up and fastened to cheap alloy buttons. In spring 1942 they were issued to the 8th Army in North Africa but were very unpopular garments and went out of fashion with no regrets.

Bombay bowler This nickname was applied to a type of sun-helmet made in India.

Bombardier This rank in the artillery is that of a junior NCO and when chevrons were introduced had but one on the right arm. In 1920 two chevrons were permitted as the rank of corporal in the artillery was abolished. Small badges of rank were worn on the

Bomb. Printed arm badge of Bomb Disposal Squads, Second World War

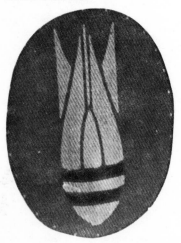

cap up to 1902 although reintroduced for arctic dress in 1944.

Bomber The term 'bomber' was introduced in the First World War for the men who threw hand-grenades. The worsted badge on the upper arm was a buff coloured ball with red flames, the officer-instructor having an all-buff grenade in his version.

Bonnet A Scottish cap. In the early days made of thick cloth, blue, black or grey. Later a knitted bonnet with a woven diced border was utilised in a variety of shapes, even to be stretched over a shako. The 'hummel' or humble bonnet could be produced as a Kilmarnock cap as still worn by the Gurkha regiments or a folded style as the glengarry worn today. Another fashion is the modern bonnet (slightly reminiscent of the beret) with a large toorie (or tourie) (q.v.) on top.

Bonnet à flamme This cap favoured by the French dragoons in the last quarter of the 17th century was a fur-edged cloth cap with the stocking-like top hanging down. Also worn by British dragoons and the horse grenadiers.

Bonnet à poil These French fur caps were worn in the 18th century by grenadiers and followed several changes of fashion as did the fur cap in the British Army.

Bonnet de police French, forage cap. These cloth caps of the Napoleonic period were for undress use and sometimes had a long tail or backpiece, usually with a tassel. They came in a variety of colours. Other shapes worn later up to modern times.

Boot cuffs These were worn by cavalrymen in the mid-18th century. They were a kind of half-stocking which went over the knees to protect them from rubbing the black of the high boots. They were usually of white cloth or cotton buttoned on to the breeches. Also called boot hose, boot-hose tops.

Booting This refers to the leather cuffs and extremities added to cavalry overalls about 1800 which continued in and out of fashion for much of the 19th century. The same leather may have continued inside the legs.

Boots Worn by cavalrymen from the earliest days of the army. Jacked leather for the largest types (hence jack-boot) which also includes the Napoleon boot. Light cavalry had shorter but stout boots until the introduction of the Hessian or hussar boot. The Wellington boot was a medium-sized boot. The Butcher boot adopted by British cavalry had a round top similar to continental types. The George boot was introduced in 1951 for the use of officers.

British infantrymen adopted half boots in 1823 when shoes were discontinued. These boots were expected to be worn alternately on either foot to give even wear. Eyelet holes had to be made to take laces. In 1838 the Cossack boot replaced these but in turn gave place to a new pattern in 1873. The handsewn boot called the Blücher was worn until 1913 when the new pattern Army ankle boot with machine-made seams was issued. Light-weight ankle boots appeared in 1932. In 1963 rubber-soled boots (directly

Boss. Types worn on front of officer's cap, f.s. coloured

Boxed epaulette. Infantry officer, c.1830

moulded soles) were to be issued. There are also special boots for special purposes like those for despatch riders and laboratory work.

Boss (a) Certain hussars had a boss on the front of the fur cap or busby. In the British forces it was usually a gold cord domed boss placed where the plume would enter the cap. It could be silver cord in the case of the yeomanry. Rifle regiments (and some light infantry) also had cord bosses of black, red and other colours on the front of the fur cap or undress cap.

(b) Hussar officers also had gold cord bosses in the notch on the front of their Hessian boots, held in place by a wire loop.

(c) Another boss is the ear boss, a metal shape at the top of the chin-scales on a headdress.

(d) Bosses are also on the browband and martingale of horse furniture.

Bowler hat This circular type of hat was used in the late 18th century and early 19th century by volunteer soldiers, who embellished them with a fur crest and feather to produce a fairly cheap military-looking headdress.

Boxed epaulettes Epaulettes (q.v.) which had a long history of evolution had hanging bullion or fringe. This frequently was damaged as it hung loosely and caught in other objects. About 1830 the idea of 'boxing' was introduced and the bullion fringe was fixed in one section so that it did not move.

Braid This woven material was used extensively on soldier's clothing. It could be plain white or yellow, as used to strengthen the brim of a hat or it could be coloured as mentioned in the 'looped clothing' of grenadiers of the Restoration period. Each button-hole was framed all round to prevent the poor cloth fraying with the buttons. The raw cut edge of the coat was also strengthened by the braid. By the middle of the 18th century the diversity of patterns served to distinguish the many infantry regiments, an idea which continued into the next century. By 1836 privates had plain white braid like the sergeants and in 1872 the many patterns of drummers' lace was reduced to two patterns, the fleur-de-lys for the Foot Guards and the red crown of line regiments. (See also 'lace'.)

Brandenburg Ornaments worn on continental clothing, froggings of braid. Although derived from Eastern costume are said to have been given the name of Brandenburgs by the French when fighting the troops of that district in 1674. The distinctive loops and fastenings were worn by hussars.

Brassard French, *bras* (arm). Band worn on the upper arm, popular in the First World War. See also Armlet, as used in modern vocabularies of clothing.

Breacan, breccan Gaelic, the plaid meaning the tartan cloth. See also belted plaid.

Breast plate The front piece of the cuirass but sometimes refers to the belt plate worn on the breast.

Breeches Lower garments which finished at the knees, fastened

Braid. Drummer of Royal Scots, *c*.1860

Brooch. For shoulder-plaid of Queen's Own Cameron Highlanders

with buttons, straps or strings. The normal nether garment in the first days of uniform until replaced by overalls or trousers for infantry. Continued in use for heavy cavalry and still worn by the Household Cavalry today.

Bren-gunners Distinguished by an arm badge with 'BG' (q.v.).

Brick dust Used by 18th-century soldiers for polishing brass fitments.

Brick red The colour of the common soldier's red coat, changed to scarlet in 1873.

Brigade This grouping of soldiers could be indicated by the wearing of a brigade sign on the shoulder in both the First and Second World Wars, when necessary. In the case of infantry in the latter conflict one, two or three strips of cloth indicated the precedence of the battalion in the brigade. After that war regiments were grouped into brigades for a short period and wore special brigade cap badges for that time.

Brigadier The officer commanding a brigade could be a brigadier or a brigadier-general. The rank distinction in Victorian times was the crossed baton and sword only, until the rank was abolished in 1920. When it returned in 1928 the badge was a crown and three stars.

Brodrick This type of cap introduced for other ranks in 1902 was named after Sir John Brodrick (later Lord Middleton), Secretary of State for War. This coloured cap was somewhat similar to the stiff service dress cap but it was without the jutting peak and it had a semi-circular piece of cloth in the front of the band in the facing colour. The Foot Guards had their own pattern of cap introduced in 1900. The Brodrick was obsolete for infantry in 1905 but it continued to be worn by the Royal Marine Light Infantry throughout the First World War.

Brogues Shoes worn by both Irish and Scots. Originally a piece of rawhide drawn into shape around the foot by a thong. In modern times a stout shoe with a tongue falling over the instep.

Broken bias The trade description for a woven metal braid or lace in which a diagonal pattern is broken with horizontal sections.

Brooch A metal fastening used by Scottish soldiers to hold the plaid in position on the shoulder. Usually circular with a stout pin at the back, the regimental badge or device in the centre. Irish pipers have their own version of the brooch to hold the shawl in place.

Browband Part of the horse's bridle which could be either of the facing colour or of metal scales.

Brunswick Star The star embroidered on the front of the cloth grenadier caps of the Foot Guards in the 18th century was called the Brunswick star although confirming evidence is lacking. The combined crosses of St George and St Andrew were within the Garter and all set on a radiating star of four points.

Brustklappen German, for the plastron on a lancer's tunic.

Buckle. For Highland dress shoes

Bugle-horn. Arm badge of Rifle Brigade, embroidered in gold thread

Brustschilder German, the metal plate or gorget carried on the chest of German cuirassiers and Garde du Corps (enamelled for officers).

Bucket The leather case on a horse for holding a carbine or a rifle.

Buckle (a) In the late seventeenth century shoe buckles were coming into fashion instead of ribbon ties. At first small and oval, they became large and square. By the 1780s strings were replacing shoe buckles but Highland regiments continued to wear the rectangular buckles, often beautifully made, right up to modern times. (b) In the mid-17th century belts had buckles, slides and tips of iron or brass. Some buckles of cavalry had sharp prongs to prevent slipping but other buckles were without in the early days. Waistbelts for sword and bayonet at the end of the 17th century had buckles which continued in use until about the middle of the next century when these belts were worn over the shoulder and took on hooked plates instead. Scottish pipers continued to have ornate buckles on their shoulder-belts. (c) Buckles were also worn at the knees of breeches (instead of strings) both of brass or cast iron. (d) Musket slings had small buckles in the 18th century made of brass with an iron tongue.

Buckskin This material, popular in the Middle Ages, made a military comeback in America in the 18th century when the garments of the Indians and trappers were adapted for rangers and other light troops. The buckskin shirt was a popular feature for the American Revolutionary soldier. Other garments were often made of the same material and proved most practical in the new type of warfare.

Buff This leather was stout and often used for the coat worn beneath a cuirass in the 17th century. It continued in use for many special guards in Europe. It was most suitable for swordbelts and also other belts which had to carry a heavy burden, yet it did not chafe the body of the wearer. Musket straps were also made of buff leather. The name is derived from the buffalo whose stout hide (and oxhide) had a soft surface.

The buff facings of certain infantry regiments refer to the colour rather than the material. As buff leather was frequently whitened, so were buff facings as in the case of the 13th Light Dragoons whose official facings were named buff although white was worn. Buff waistcoat and breeches worn by infantry men in the 18th century referred to the colour not the material.

Bugle This as an arm badge is not necessarily that of a bugler but may also indicate light infantry.

Buglehorn The badge of a buglehorn is frequently confused with that of the bugle and the powder horn. An animal horn could be used as a bugle but the normal bugle is a long metal horn which was curled to make a shorter instrument, either in a circle as for cavalry and hunting or an oval shape as for infantry. Double bugle-horns (cow horns with strings) are worn over the NCOs stripes in a rifle or light infantry regiment.

Busby. Officer of 18th Hussars

Bugler This infantry musician although carrying a bugle, in the British Army is also a drummer and wears the badge of a drum on his upper arm (see also drummer). In America the metal bugle is worn as the arm badge as it is in some European countries. In British rifle regiments the drum is not used for field calls and therefore the bugler wears the badge of the stringed horn, a feature of riflemen since 1800.

Bullion This is the name given to gold and silver wire (or ribbon) made into a continuous hollow spiral. Large bullion on epaulettes was considered more elegant than fringe. Small lengths of bullion were couched for ornamentation on sabretaches, pouches and other items of the lacemaker's craft.

Bummers' cap Fatigue or forage caps of the American Civil War were later called 'bummers' caps' when worn by Sherman's Bummers in Georgia.

Burnside hat A variety of the black hat worn in the American Civil War was the 'Burnside', a low-crowned version which looped up on the right side.

Büsche German for musket, rifle or carbine.

Busby This name given to fur caps in the British Army had its origins in an English military supplier. W. Busby of the Strand, London also provided the fur caps for hussar officers when these cavalrymen became part of the British Army about 1805. The term originally only applied to the fur caps worn by hussars and horse artillery but may now be used for the Royal Engineers and the Royal Corps of Signals full dress headdress. It does not apply to the fur caps of the Foot Guards, nor any caps which derive from the fur caps of grenadiers.

Busby bag The original cap worn by hussars was likened to a long jelly bag which had a narrow edging of fur. When the fur grew in height to hide the cloth the bag fell freely. But it eventually became fixed and flat on the right side, with braid in the case of hussars or plain in the artillery. Originally the hussars favoured the colour of red for the bag although the 18th Hussars had a light blue until they were disbanded in 1821. As light dragoons were converted to hussars new colours appeared for busby bags. The re-raised 18th Hussars had a 'green fly' as the Dress Regulation stated but this later changed to blue. The new 19th, 20th and 21st Hussars had respectively white, crimson and French grey. See also 'bag'.

Bush hat This broad-brimmed hat introduced for tropical wear no doubt had its origins in the type worn by African hunters or the Australian 'bushwhackers'. It was worn extensively in the Second World War in the Far East and the Middle East, frequently with the side turned up, where a badge and/or a formation sign could be worn.

Bush shirt This khaki drill shirt, also inspired by civilian fashion, could be considered as a type of tunic for it had side pockets on the skirts. For an uncomfortable period troops in the Middle East had

33

Buttons. Royal Horse Guards *c.*1790, 3rd Buffs *c.*1803, 46th Foot *c.*1820, 30th Cambridge *c.*1840

Buttons. Royal Horse Guards *c.*1790, 3rd Buffs *c.*1803, 46th Foot *c.*1820, 30th Cambridge *c.*1840

to wear the bulky skirts tucked inside the shorts but later when permitted outside the bush shirt was a cool and comfortable garment. It was worn with an open neck, frequently with a 'sweat rag'.

Butternut The term referred to the colour of the Confederate uniforms in the American Civil War. The dye ranged from yellow to dark brown and was produced from nut-shells boiled with iron oxide or copper.

Button The information on buttons worn by soldiers could (and does) fill many books, and all aspects cannot be covered here. Officers' buttons followed a different line of development from those of other ranks. The thread buttons of officers usually laid over a wooden mould. Gold or silver thread made special patterns which were later imitated when gold or silver sheet replaced the thread. Instead of the wooden core, ivory or bone was used with holes through to take the thread. Later an all-metal button was produced with a fixed metal shank.

Other ranks had metal buttons in the mid-18th century either of pewter or brass. It was not until 1767 that British buttons were numbered or given regimental distinctions. The flat engraved button gave place to a cast type and as the shape became more domed, the shank became longer. About 1830 closed buttons of two pieces were being made. Metal ball buttons were worn by hussars and light cavalry. These were usually plain but later a design or letters were engraved. Black composition buttons were worn by early rifle corps and are worn today by Gurkha regiments.

There are many materials for buttons, composition and brown leather worn with service dress were authorised in 1917. There were different buttons for battle dress and fighting dress, elegant buttons for mess dress as well as those worn by the mess waiters, to say nothing of non-regulation items which might have been produced abroad, specially in India. Aluminium anodysed buttons were designed in 1947 and came into use several years later.

Button-holes That holes should have any significance may seem a strange thought but in the army they were a form of distinction. The cloth of soldiers' clothing in the early days of the Standing Army was very thin, and button-holes needed strengthening to prevent wear by the sharp buttons. Therefore the holes were strengthened with loops of braid or lace (q.v. loop). These braids developed regimental patterns and colours. Holes and button-holes were also worn in pairs. Officers had gold or silver lace on their holes or in inexpensively inclined regiments embroidered holes. Today the Foot Guards may be distinguished by the grouping of their buttons which are regular for the Grenadier Guards, in pairs for the Coldstream Guards, in threes for the Scots Guards, in fours for the Irish Guards and in fives for the Welsh Guards.

C

c. Embroidered on khaki for qualified cook

C The initial 'c' is used to indicate the 'c' group of tradesmen (see also 'A') and is in the usual laurel wreath. This trade group became obsolete in 1950. A block letter 'c' also in laurel leaves is said to have been worn by qualified cooks. It was in use before the 'c' trade categories were created but disappeared soon after.

Caban This was a very loose overcoat, almost a shaped cloak of heavy cloth lined with red worn by French officers, inspired by the North African campaigns of the 1830s and 1840s. It was worn instead of the 'redingote' and cloak.

Cadet When under training cadets frequently wore a uniform like that of an officer but without the badges of rank. At the Royal Military Academy and the Royal Military College the uniform of the Royal Artillery and that of the infantry of the Line was worn but with NCOs markings when necessary and special distinctions for cadet ranking.

Cadet gray In the early part of the 19th century the United States Army Cadets at West Point wore a grey uniform. This cadet grey was worn by the regular infantry when material was scarce, thus leading the enemy to consider that the troops may have been volunteers or untrained only to be rudely awakened in following engagements.

Calotte French. Before the steel helmet was generally introduced in the First World War the French infantry were issued with *calottes* or covers which were expected to be worn under the kepi. The *calotte* was a steel coif worn under the cavalry hat at the end of the 17th century, perhaps taking its name from the skull cap of a priest.

Camisole French, an undercoat or long waistcoat popular in the 18th century.

Camouflage French, meaning a disguise, popular during the First World War when broken patches of colour were applied to cannon, vehicles, helmets and buildings. In the Second World War loose smocks or jackets in camouflage colours were worn, also loose trousers in the same fashion. These colour schemes varied according to the theatres of war.

Camouflage net Painting of headdress was not sufficient to break up the outline. A covering of wide mesh netting (also in camouflage colours) served to hold the natural foliage of the area of operation.

Cane Lengths of bamboo or rattan were made into short sticks (q.v. stick) carried by soldiers, both officers (specially in the First World War) and men (for walking out). Still carried today in the Household Cavalry, although generally discontinued during the Second World War.

Cannon A badge as early as 1821 used on its own to mark artillerymen. Crossed gun or cannon barrels also worn above rank badges to indicate skill, prize or appointment like AIG (q.v.).

Canteen A vessel to hold water or for cooking utensils.

Cantiniére French. Women who carried a canteen of water or spirits for the benefit of soldiers during battle, wore a special uniform, a combination of female dress and soldiers' uniform. Although officially allowed in Continental armies, were not so in the British Army. Occasionally wives of soldiers were permitted to undertake sutlery and to wear a military coat.

Canvas This strong unbleached cloth of hemp or flax (known under various names like ravenduck (q.v.) was used for fatigue clothes, trousers in particular from 1807 and no doubt earlier. Canvas smocks were worn for laboratory work in the artillery. In 1902 canvas clothing was introduced to save the khaki uniforms. Worn in the First World War in white, were replaced by brown canvas suits until denims were introduced.

Cap Caput, capo means head and the cap is normally a small item, as opposed to a hat which has a brim all round. A cap may have a peak or not and is applied to very many shapes. The shako was also called a cap. A watering cap could be of leather or other stout material. The forage cap was found with a wide soft top or made stiff. The cap f.s. (field service) could be folded flat. The cap g.s. (general service) was an imitation of a beret in cloth but not so well formed.

Cap bands In the US Army, the peaked cap had coloured bands to indicate the arm of service. In the early 20th century, staff officers had a black band while the distinction for cavalry was yellow, light blue for infantry, red for artillery, red and white for engineers, etc. Officers had gold edging top and bottom of the band whereas enlisted men had black bands with top and bottom edging of the distinctive colours.

Cap comforter The khaki woollen scarf worn in the First World War was a flattened tube which could be turned up and down on the head to simulate a cap, thus providing the cap comforter.

Cap (holster) The attachment in the front of the cavalry saddle

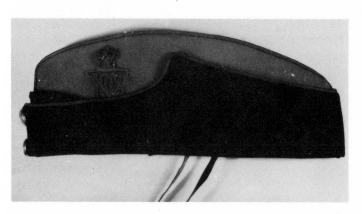

Cap. Field service. Officer, 5th Dragoon Guards

in the 18th century had flaps or covers known as caps. These were regulated by the orders which affected the horsecloth or shabraque and had regimental devices and lace.

Cap-lines These lines or cords are worn with a cap (such as a lance-cap) so that being fixed around the neck and the cap, the headdress would not be lost when the wearer was on horseback. They were frequently fastened according to a regimental practice (as were the busby lines of hussars).

Cape (a) In the 18th century the word cape frequently referred to the turned-down collar on a coat. (b) Some cloaks for cavalry in the 19th and 20th centuries had capes on the shoulders. Infantry coats also had the addition of capes at certain periods.

Captain In the 16th century infantry groups were under the command of a captain but later the rank of captain was reduced to the command of a single company and below the rank of a field officer. In the early 19th century the rank of a captain was indicated by a single epaulette on the right shoulder, although captains of grenadier companies and fusiliers wore two wings. See also rank badges.

Carabine, carabin Variations of carbine (q.v.).

Carbine A shortened firearm mainly used by cavalrymen. Regiments of carabiniers were raised in England and on the continent in the late 17th century. The descendants of one such regiment became known as the 6th Dragoon Guards (Carabiniers) and wore the badge of crossed carbines on the uniform and horse furniture.

Cartouche Another spelling of cartridge, the combined bullet and powder in paper (or later in a metal case). Also referring to the small box to hold same.

Cartridge belt A belt to hold cartridges usually worn over the shoulder. The cartridges could be in pouches grouped in sets as in the leather pattern of each in single loops as on the web belt.

Cartridge box The introduction of the made-up cartridge brought into use a box to hold same. It could be worn from a shoulder belt or on a waistbelt. A large over-lapping flap on top protected the cartridges from the weather but it could be easily raised by the hand which extracted the cartridge. Variations included a tin box inside the leather pouch or much later a wooden block pierced with holes to hold cartridges.

Casque French. Helmet or head-piece, ranging from early knightly days up to the Adrian tinhat of modern days.

Casquette French. A cap of various shapes, also a peaked shako.

Casque-à-chenille French helmet with a 'caterpillar', i.e. the crest covering the top of a metal helmet either of silk or wool. Popular in Napoleonic times but also worn later in German states (see Raupenhelme).

Casque-à-point French helmet with a point or spike.

Cassock A long outer coat worn by cavalry and infantry, popular in the 17th century. Often worn open with wide turn-up on the

Carbine. Crossed carbines on badge of 6th Carabiniers (Dragoon Guards)

Castle. Badge of Dorsetshire Regiment

sleeves.

Castle Popular as a badge in British regiments which achieved fame in the Great Siege of Gibraltar when the castle and key is worn. During the siege the keys to the enemy's arsenal were captured but the reason for its adoption on the badge seems to be the fact that Gibraltar was the 'key' to the Mediterranean. As many regiments are associated with castles in their home towns these appear as a badge, i.e. Edinburgh Castle, the castles of Exeter, Inniskillin, Suffolk and Northampton. American engineers have the badge of a castle to demonstrate their work, rather than a place.

Castor Obsolete word for beaver. Hats were made of this fur. Pepys in 1661 speaks of these as a novelty and officers wore same.

Category badge Arm badges worn by certain categories of tradesmen etc.

Cath d'ath Scottish, cloth hose (q.v. hose).

Cavalry star-loop When the helmet was superseding the hat in heavy cavalry the more ancient hat was retained for levées and certain full-dress occasions. These hats had an elaborate gold or silver embroidered star instead of the smaller button and loop. There were certain distinctive loops for some regiments like the Royal Horse Guards and the Fifth Dragoon Guards.

Ceinture French sash, girdle or belt.

Centry gown The name given for the watch coat in Charles II's reign. The centinel or sentinel coats were limited in issue to those for night duty or bad weather and were not general issue.

Cert. A The Certificate 'A', awarded to proficient cadets, was marked by a red silken star worn on the right arm (a half star for Part One only).

Cert. T The Technical certificate for Cadets introduced in the Second World War was marked by a khaki four-pointed star worn on the right arm.

Chaco, chako, chakot Other spellings for shako (q.v.).

Chain gimp The type of gimp or braid in silver or gold was popular for decorating the uniforms of hussars. Black gimp was used for rifle units.

Chains Modern use of the word for shoulder-chains (q.v.) of cavalry. Also foot-chains worn under the instep by cavalrymen to retain the spurs in position.

Chambary Russian, bright red leather trousers, 19th century.

Chape, or crampet The end of a leather scabbard or the end of a belt.

Chapeau French. A hat. When the shako came into use in the United States, the chapeau or cocked hat continued a ceremonial or staff hat until 1936.

Chapeau bras French flattened hat, capable of being carried under the arm, popular for levées, balls, etc.

Chapkan, chapken An Indian coat.

Chapplis Sandals worn by Indian foot soldiers in the 18th and 19th centuries.

Chevron. Sergeant's chevrons on khaki drill

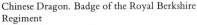
Chinese Dragon. Badge of the Royal Berkshire Regiment

Chapska From the Turkish, *tschapka, shapka, schapska*. Lance-cap (q.v.).

Charivara, charawaden, scharawader, esquavar Continental hussars of the 18th century wore short leather breeches with the *charivara* (woollen leg pieces) over the knees and up to the thighs. They were not in use in the British cavalry.

Charjama A thick saddlecloth used by Indian cavalry in the 19th century.

Checkers or dicing The small squares worn on Scottish head-dresses.

Chèches French. The head covering worn by most North African troops in the French service. The colours differed according to the squadrons or battalions, but on service all chèches were khaki.

Chéchia French officers never wore the *chèche*, but they did wear the *chéchia*, a soft fez-like cap with a tassel. Also worn by zouaves and tirailleurs.

Cheekpieces The ornaments either side of a horse's bridle.

Chevron Heraldically a chevron is a 'V' shape with the point to the top. In the late 18th century French soldiers wore chevrons as a badge for long service. Occasional use of chevrons or bars in the British Army indicated a soldier with long service as an NCO. In 1803 a system of rank marking was introduced for British NCOs. A sergeant-major and quartermaster-sergeant wore four chevrons, a sergeant three and a corporal two. Some regiments according to contemporary prints wore the chevron point upwards but an order of May 1803 stated 'point downward'. Chevrons were worn on patches of the facing colour but when khaki was introduced, buff on khaki became general. Chevrons are also called 'stripes'. Originally chevrons were worn on the upper arm but in 1869 the four of the sergeant major were worn on the lower sleeve with the points towards the elbow. Service stripes (q.v.) are chevrons worn on the left forearm as were the small wound stripes when they were introduced in time of war.

Chin-chain Full dress shakos and helmets had chin-chains in the 19th century. Leather straps and scale straps had been worn previously. The chin-chains were made of circular overlapping links flattened on a leather strap.

Chinese Dragon This distinctive badge was worn by regiments which served in China 1840–2, like the 49th Foot, also the 18th, 26th, 34th and 98th.

Chin-scales Cavalry helmets and shakos had chin-straps of overlapping and diminishing scales in the early 19th century but changed over to chin-chains.

Chitterlin The small shirt frill seen at the opening of the neck.

Choga, chogga Indian great coat of camelhair with portion for covering the head.

Cholera belt These flannel belts were introduced mid-19th century with the idea of preventing cholera. Worn around the

Coat. Officer of the 3rd Foot Guards, *c.1773*

Coatee. Sergeant, 80th Foot, *c.1830*

waist and under outer garments in China and other places in the Far East in the early 20th century. Later patterns were of thick wool and pulled on.

Chupkan, chapkan A type of Indian coat.

Clasp The fastening for the stock which went around the neck was a clasp.

Cloak The sleeveless cloak worn by cavalrymen was of such dimensions that it covered the back part of the horse furniture and the horse itself. Heavy cavalry, hussars and light dragoons in 1841 had sleeves added to their cloaks but these were cancelled almost at once. About 20 years later sleeves were again added and included the Royal Horse Artillery.

Cloathing, clothing Refers to the garments worn by the common soldier. Even in the 20th century military indices for privates' uniform is listed under 'clothing' but that of officers under 'dress'.

Coat The doublet or upper garment gave place to the coat. As a long garment at the end of the 17th century (perhaps called a cassock) it was the main outer garment of the common soldier worn over a waistcoat. It was not substantial for wear or warmth and at night a watchcoat (q.v. centry gown) was worn. The lining or facing of early coats was usually of a different colour. Thus when the long sleeves were turned back, the facing appeared. Collars when turned down also showed the facing colour, as did the fronts of the coat when turned back as lapels. At the end of the 18th century the coat had become shortened and finally closed down the front leaving the once-ample skirts as little more than ornaments behind. In 1855 the coatee was replaced by the tunic (q.v. collar and cuff).

Coat, buff (see also buff) At the Restoration horse troopers wore buff coats, relics of the days of armour, but the reign of James II saw the buff leather coat as little more than a protection against sword cuts and no value against firearms; they thus became no more than waistcoats.

Coat, blanket (see also blanket coat) In America in particular blankets were made into a coat shape, no doubt making a popular nondescript garment favoured by the many deserters quoted in the papers of the day.

Coatee Meaning a small coat, referring to the 19th century body garments closed in front and cut across the waist leaving only small skirts behind. The style of garment was still referred to as a coat in the beginning but by the time of the Crimean War was officially called a coatee.

Cochineal The brilliant red dye used for the Foot Guards coats in Queen Victoria's reign came from the cochineal bug. These insects flourished in Mexico, Peru and southern Spain. In Spain this dye had been used as early as 1580. Modern synthetic dyes are not only cheaper but are simpler to use.

Cockade The need for national colours in the continental wars of the 18th century brought about, not only distinctive uniforms, but national cockades. When the brim of the hat was needed to be caught up on the side, ribbons were used. Although black was a convenient colour some nations took the opportunity to show their own colour – Bavaria did so in 1702. George I gave his British troops black cockades to be different from the white one of the Stuarts. The Black Watch are known to have had red for a period. The emergent United States combined black with the white of the French as a compliment. However, national ideas were forgotten when ranks were shown by coloured cockades, red or pink for field officers, yellow for captains and green for subalterns. The black cockade remained in use for British troops even on the few cocked hats of today. The red, white and blue of France, the red, white and black of Germany are well known as headdress cockades and the list of other nations is extensive.

In the early days of the American Revolution distinctions of officers were indicated by the colour of the cockades in the hat – red or pink for captains, green for subalterns.

Cocked hat The broad-brimmed hat of Carolian days had a flat brim but occasionally one side might have been curled to keep it in position in wet or windy weather. When two sides were curled up as in William and Mary's time this made a horn or cocked corner. When the third part was turned up a hat with three cocked corners appeared. Even these were pushed about before the end of the century when the front cock was pushed up so high as to leave only two corners at the sides thus making the tricorne into a bicorne. The cocked hat now developed into a flat hat which could be carried under the arm (q.v. *chapeu-à-bras*). The stiff cocked hat (popular with the Royal Navy) was now worn 'fore-and-aft' for high ranking officers in the Army or for those departments like engineers and medical services. Today the quarter-masters of the Foot Guards still wear the cocked hat, as do the officers of the Pensioners, Royal Hospital, Chelsea. The Pensioners themselves are the last to wear the three-cornered cocked hat.

Cocks'-feathers These curled feathers which replaced the ostrich feathers worn in the cocked hats of general officers at the start of the 19th century, were used to ornament headdresses of general officers, lancers, light dragoons, rifle officers and yeomanry. Black plumes were popular but white over red was a staff distinction. The shape on the cocked hat being rather like a ball. See also swans' feathers.

Collar All coats did not have collars and in the 17th century the large white shirt collar sufficed. A short standing collar about one inch high appeared on buff coats. This fashion continued on the cloth coat of the mid-18th century but by the time of the American Revolution the falling collar was gaining popularity in the army. In the peace that followed collars rose to the stand and fall fashion. About 1788 the 'fall' part was omitted and the stiff standing part was ornamented with lace or braid. When the coat closed down the front, the collar still retained its 'v' opening from which the shirt frill appeared. The closed or Prussian collar appeared about 1820 in the British Army, and remained with little modification throughout the life of full dress.

Collar, silver The 3rd Dragoons (later 3rd Light Dragoons and 3rd Hussars) had an interesting custom for their kettledrummer. As the drummer in the late 18th century was a negro slave he was given a silver collar by the colonel's wife, an item which continues in wear to the present day.

Collar-maker The trade of collar-maker (for horses) was distinguished by the arm badge of a cavalry bit (q.v. bit).

Collar button or insignia These circular devices worn in the US Army served to indicate the arm of service, actual unit or even trade of the wearer. They replaced the larger brass collar ornaments and badges about the time of the First World War.

Colonel When badges of rank were introduced for officers the colonel in 1810 wore a crown and star on each epaulette up to the Crimean War and then the same on the collar. After 1881 when rank badges were moved to the shoulder-cords, a crown and two stars was worn by a full colonel, one star less for a lieutenant-colonel.

Colouring Unfortunately items as officially issued were not always as the regiments wished and local additions like colouring were introduced. In 1881 when so many regiments were given white facings, the Buffs wished to retain their ancient facings and so coloured the white buff. Today equipment is often coloured differently, that of the Royal Tank Regiment being black. Frequently the unofficial method became official.

Colours In the Army the Colours are the regimental 'flags'. The word flag is considered to refer to the naval and fixed position item and the word 'colours' dates back to the 16th century when flags of many coloured strips and pieces were carried by the infantry. The badge of crossed colours was worn by the colour-sergeant (q.v.) until the recruiting service took it over.

Colour-sergeant The rank of colour-sergeant was introduced into the British army in 1813 when it was wished to give some reward to senior sergeants of good standing. The first colour badge to be worn on the arms was a single Union colour with crossed swords below on the staff. Certain regiments produced their own version, those known today being the Foot Guards each of whom have their regimental 'red' colour. In 1868 the pattern changed to two crossed Union colours without swords but still the crown above as well as the three chevrons. In 1915 the colour-sergeants' badge disappeared although it re-appeared for the recruiting service (q.v.). The Foot Guards continue their own version with varying crowns as the pattern change.

Combat clothing This is self-explanatory but in modern times it refers to a loose smock or overall garment, frequently camouflaged and other strong clothing intended for rough field work.

Colour-sergeant. Arm badge, c.1865

Communications In the Middle Ages the voice of a knight was sufficient to give instructions to his men but the growth of command (and the din of battle) led to 'middlemen', the drummers who tapped the commands and the trumpeters who sounded their versions of the calls. Further distance brought in signallers, both the visual type with flags and the electric contacts by telephone, telegraph and wireless. All these professional soldiers have their trades (see under appropriate heading). The coming of radar increased the trades and in some cases a simplification of categories had to be made as when the operator w/l had to enter the wider anonymous group of 'B' tradesmen.

Cook A cook may be readily distinguished in his duties when he or she wears white clothing and a white hat. In service dress for a time the letter 'c' within laurels was the arm badge but when grouping was introduced the cook then belonged to the 'B' group and wore that badge.

Cords On the headdress of the United States Army, cords are noted in the 1861 uniform regulations as distinguishing enlisted men by being in the colour of the facings of their respective corps, a fashion which continued in use.

Cork helmet In India the ordinary helmet or shako was oppressive and sweat-producing. In the middle of the 19th century lightweight sun helmets were introduced. Wicker covered with cloth was tried but cork was found to be more satisfactory. In 1939 officers began wearing the pith helmet, originally a civilian head-covering.

Cornet The lowest rank of officer in cavalry was the cornet. Originally he was expected to carry the cornet (flag) of the troop. But as in the case of the infantry the number of flags per regiment was reduced and so also the cornet-carrying duties. Then cavalry flags changed their names and the cornet as such disappeared although the rank continued in the British Army until 1871 when it was abolished. A single star was worn on the collar as a badge of rank from 1855 to 1871.

Coronation Blues As full dress for 'other ranks' had not been restored after the First World War, a certain dilemma arose at the Coronation of 1937. Blue tunics and trousers were produced only for the soldiers taking part in the procession. In fact there was a dark green uniform for rifle regiments but the term 'Coronation Blues' was the popular expression.

Corporal This rank, which comes below that of a sergeant, had little distinction in early times. Whereas the sergeant often had cloth of a better quality the corporal had the men's clothing with the addition of braid or a shoulder-knot. When chevrons were introduced in 1803 two chevrons were authorised and are still worn today.

Corselet This word refers to the cuirass (or back and breast plate) worn by cavalry officers but C. Walton includes gorgets in this description. Term obsolete before end of 17th century.

Cork Helmet. With cover, Royal Artillery, c.1899

Cravat This type of neckcloth became popular in the British Army in the last quarter of the 17th century. The word derives from Croat, *krabate*, the people who preferred a piece of cloth around the neck instead of the falling band. Men of the Foot Guards in 1678 had 'cravatts of fox-tails' the ends of which were tied with scarlet ribbon. 'Fox-tail' appears to apply to the ornamental ends of the cravat which could have been indented or laced. In the 1680s the cravat strings were discontinued and by the early 1690s the 'Steenkirk' was in fashion.

In modern warfare specially in hot climates the sweat-rag is worn as introduced in the 1939–45 War. In Korea US troops favoured pleated cravats in corps colours. In the present time British troops have adopted coloured cravats for wear with certain arctic service clothing.

Crescent When the epaulette developed into a more ornate affair a solid metal crescent was worn at the shoulder end of the strap to go above the fringe or bullion. The all-metal shoulder-scales worn on officers' undress coats or by cavalrymen in the second quarter of the 19th century also had metal crescents.

An unusual use of the crescent was in the case of the belt ornament of the officers of the 10th Foot *c.*1800 which had a silver plate engraved with the regimental number instead of the usual belt-plate.

The crescent occasionally appeared in band badges of the early 19th century to denote the Turkish influence on musical instruments.

Crest The crest on ancient helmets could be of feather or horse-hair. When in the early 19th century helmets again became popular, those of Grecian or Roman pattern had animal or vegetable ornaments on top known as the crest. In the British Army the heavy cavalry had silken or woollen crests, sometimes called caterpillars (see *casque-à-chenille* and *raupenhelme*).

The medieval helmet crest had an heraldic significance and frequently developed into un-natural shapes. The crest became part of the coat-of-arms of a knightly person. Although not always regally approved, crests of non-royal persons appears as regimental badges as in the case of the Ligonier crest for the 7th Dragoon Guards and the Duke of Wellington's crest for the 33rd Regiment of Foot.

Cross Apart from having a Christian significance the cross has always been popular as a device or symbol. The cross of St George, of St Andrew and of St Patrick frequently appear on British badges. But the Maltese cross (q.v.) (of eight slender points) is said to have been introduced the Hompesch who raised the Fifth battalion of the King's Rifle Corps and may have been related to Hompesch the last Grand Master of the Maltese Order of St John. Rifle regiments favour as a badge the Maltese cross or rather the cross patée into which it has developed. This cross was also worn by cavalry men in the 1830s on helmet and sabretache.

Cross. St Andrew's cross on badge of 79th Highlanders

Cross-belt Waistbelts had been worn by infantrymen in the early 18th century to carry both sword and bayonet, but cavalrymen favoured the baldrick or shoulder-belt for the sword. The large cartridge pouch was carried on a belt over the left shoulder, thus making cross-belts a style which did not reach the infantry until about 1780 and continued up to most of the next century. The 8th Dragoons (later 8th Hussars) in 1710 captured many belts from the enemy and wore them with the sword-belts thus acquiring the nickname of the 'Cross-belts'.

Cross pocket Pocket flaps on the 18th-century coats were horizontal but the shortening of the skirts and removal of cloth towards the back brought about the use of vertical pockets. The introduction of the jacket at the end of the century with very short tails left space only for small 'cross' (horizontal) pockets.

Crown Great Britain being a monarchy included the badge of a crown when badges of rank were introduced. Thus the crown being a royal symbol takes precedence over the star. The crown also appeared on the arms of NCOs of Household Cavalry. It appears over the stripes and other rank badges of NCOs.

Crowsfoot The ornaments of three loops (either of embroidery or lace) were considered to be like a 'crowsfoot'. They appeared on the turnback of skirts when they were held with a hook and eye. The term also applies to the 'trefoil' which might appear on a cuff or elsewhere traced in cord, braid or embroidery.

Cuff The cuff developed from the long sleeve which reached down to cover the knuckles and when turned back to display the facing colour, had buttons to keep it up. Although the buttoning may have been temporary at first, the buttoning back became permanent. During the process, various methods of fastening took place. One with a long side slash developing into the buttoned flap worn today by the Foot Guards. The simple round cuff with buttons at the top is known as the 'Swedish' cuff. The one with a pointed cuff and a button at the top is the 'Polish' cuff. The British 'round' cuff was usually without buttons but this gave place in the infantry to a pointed cuff without any button. Cavalry and corps usually favour a pointed cuff ornamented with an Austrian knot, a trefoil (crowsfoot) or an even more elaborate knot.

Cuirass Apart from the helmet the cuirass afforded the best protection to the warrior. The pikeman continued to wear the cuirass up to the end of the 17th century. Regiments of horse at the time of the Restoration wore the helmet and cuirass but by 1675 it was usual to wear the breastpiece only. The cuirass was discontinued for everyday use but kept in store and drawn out for campaigns like those of Marlborough, the Seven Years' War and the Netherlands campaign of 1794, for service use only. On the continent the cuirass was still worn and in 1814 when Napoleon abdicated a Royal Review was held in Hyde Park and for the occasion a subdivision of the 2nd Life Guards appeared in ceremonial cuirasses. In 1821 the King determined that both the Life

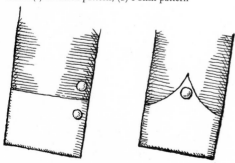

Cuffs. (a) Swedish pattern, (b) Polish pattern

Cycle wheel. Embroidered arm badge early 20th
century

Cypher. Normal Queen Victoria and reversed cypher

Guards and the Royal Horse Guards would wear cuirasses and these appeared at the Coronation on 19 July. After minor variations in design, cuirasses are still worn today by the Household Cavalry on State occasions.

Cummerbund, cummerband, kamarband The Indian cavalry introduced the cummerbund to British officers. When first worn in India it served to keep the netherwear in place, while a light upper garment could be worn in mess or at balls and parties. Troops serving in India adopted the cummerbund without official guidance but in 1954 (after we had departed from India) they were permitted for mess dress. Sergeants and other NCOs also were given permission for mess wear.

The long piece of cotton, silk or muslin was wound round the waist many times but simpler versions have appeared. The colours permitted for mess dress include, for example, scarlet for staff and senior officers, all yellow for the 4th Hussars, black and white for the 9th Lancers, pearl grey for the Royal Leicestershire Regiment, rose for the Lancashire Fusiliers and tartan for the Scottish regiments.

Curran These simple shoes once worn in Scotland and Ireland were made from soft leather drawn up by a thong to the ankle. The early Scottish soldiers like the Black Watch wore these until the more solid brogue (q.v.) developed.

Cycle wheel This badge embroidered in buff on khaki was an arm badge for trained cyclists in the early 20th century but it soon disappeared when the motor-cycle appeared.

Cyclist In the late 19th century the improved cycle seemed to be the ideal 'steed' for infantry scouts. Companies and battalions were formed for reconnaissance purposes and with the idea of rapid transference of infantrymen to special places of attack. Mobile machine-guns were drawn by cycles but message carrying was a more practical task. Many cyclist battalions were attached to divisions in the First World War wearing their own cap badges (usually including a cycle wheel in the design) but the end of the war saw the last of these battalions.

Cypher It was the custom in olden days for sovereigns and certain nobility to form their initials into a monogram. The interlinking letters sometimes included reversed letters and present a code or cypher for unravelling. These distinctive cyphers were worn on coats of musicians and horse furniture. The State dress of the Household Cavalry musicians still bears the initials of the Sovereign. The ornamental horse furniture has all but disappeared and the cypher remains most obviously on metal cap badges.

Czapska (see chapka) The Polish cap with four sides originally favoured by the people of Cracow which was the inspiration for lancers' caps.

D

Diver. Arm badge for diver

Divisional sign. 56th Armoured Division

D The letter 'D' with laurel sprays is the badge for group 'D' tradesmen. (See also 'A', 'B' and 'C'.)

Dannebrog The Danish Cross borne on the Danish national flag and brought into the British Army by Queen Alexander, Danish wife of King Edward VII. She granted this cross to the 19th Hussars in 1872 and to the 19th Foot (later the Green Howards) in 1879 when she became their colonel-in-chief. The Dannebrog and the appropriate dates appear on the cap badges.

DEMS These letters stand for 'defensively equipped merchant ships' and were worn on the shoulders of the men of the Maritime Regiment, Royal Artillery in the last war.

De Nimes The place of origin in France for denims (q.v.).

Denims The name given to a stout hard-wearing suit worn on fatigue duties. Adopted in the British Army in modern times when the canvas suit went out of use.

Diced band, diced border, dicing Woven or sewn pattern of squares on Scottish bonnets and headdresses. Had its origin in a drawstring threaded through holes in the band but soon became an ornamental vestige. Usually of three rows varying in colour; red and white for Sutherland Highlanders; red, white and green; red, white and blue; blue and white and other combinations.

Dienstanzug German. Dress for duty or service.

Dienstgradabzeichen German rank badges.

Dienstdecke German saddlecloth.

Dienstmutze German service cap.

Dirk A dagger much used in the Middle Ages and still worn by Scottish soldiers. Handle usually of bogwood with a cairngorm set on the top. Blade elaborately engraved in the case of officers. The black scabbard has the addition of a small fork and knife, also set with cairngorms. Pipers and others have a simpler version.

Dirk belt The waistbelt to suspend the sheathed dirk may have a frog (q.v.) for suspension and a pad also. The dirk is placed over the right thigh.

Distance Judging A soldier proficient in distance judging (for the use of a firearm or larger weapon) was granted an arm badge of an embroidered star. This was worn on the right forearm above other badges.

Diver The qualified diver is permitted the arm badge of a diver's helmet. A diver qualified for diving in shallow water wears the helmet with 'sw' below (introduced c.1953). In the Second World War divers were attached to commandos for special duties.

Divisional signs The wearing of regimental badges and insignia in the First World War led the enemy to deduce troop movements and strength. The use of obscure divisional signs which gave no

Doublet. Other rank of 93rd Foot, full dress, c.1880

clear information of units or strength began on vehicles but soon appeared on the clothing of the fighting man. These cabalistic marks were revived in the Second World War and continued in use after the war. Other nations adopted the British custom. The origins can be seen in the Crimean War and the American Civil War armies.

DM These letters appear as an arm badge with the usual laurels to indicate a Driver Mechanic of the between-war periods.

Dogs 'Collar dogs' is the slang expression for collar badges.

Dolman Worn on the continent by light cavalrymen, called a jacket in Britain. Developed from the caftan and replaced by the attila (q.v.) after 1860 in German and other armies.

Doublet Originally a civilian garment evolved into a 'four-tailed' coat. In Scotland it developed gauntlet cuffs and ornamental skirt-flaps. In the case of Scottish pipers the doublet was not red but blue or green with ornamental wings of patterns which varied with the unit and the years.

Don R Slang for DR, despatch rider on motor cycle.

DR Initials in laurels for the arm badge of the despatch rider, now obsolete.

Drab The colour by which khaki was known when a service colour was adopted in the British Army. Derives from the French *drap* meaning cloth.

Dragon Being a Royal badge from Tudor times it is still worn as a cap badge in Welsh regiments. The Buffs wore the dragon with a claim going back to Queen Elizabeth I, who had the dragon as a supporter to her arms. The Northumberland Fusiliers had an ancient claim to the dragon being slain by St George. Troops who distinguished themselves in China had the Chinese dragon (q.v.) as a badge.

Dragonne de sabre French. Sword knot.

Dragoon Originally an infantryman mounted on a poor type of horse, mainly for conveyance to the place where he was expected to dismount and fight. It is said that the flaming match for his musket was reminiscent of a dragon, hence his name. He later remained on his horse to fight as a light cavalryman with either his sword or his firearm. The dragoon dress became a modification of that of heavier cavalry and most dragoon regiments converted to either light dragoons, hussars or lancers. By the time of Waterloo, only the 1st, 2nd, 3rd, 4th and 6th Dragoons remained wearing the red coat. By 1818 the 3rd and 4th had been converted leaving only the Royal Dragoons, the Royal Scots Greys and the Inniskillin Dragoons to be the last mounted dragoons, all of which are now amalgamated into new regiments.

Dragoon Guards Regiments of horse (the normal cavalry) were considered to be too ponderous in the field, so in 1746 three regiments were converted to dragoon guards, a new term which meant that they were paid little more than the dragoon. They retained the red coat as worn from earliest day until the end of full

Dragon. Badge of the Buffs

dress. Four more regiments of horse were converted in 1788. Of the seven regiments of dragoon guards, one (the 6th) was due for conversion to light dragoons and took a blue uniform. Actually the change did not take place but the blue uniform was retained by the Carabiniers. After Waterloo dragoon guards were distinguished from dragoons by the former wearing velvet facings and the latter cloth. The Albert helmet of Dragoon Guards introduced about 1847 was gilt or brass while that for Dragoons was silver or white metal.

Dress This normally refers to the uniform worn by officers as opposed to the 'clothing' (q.v.) worn by the men. Thus the Dress Regulations which were printed from 1822 onwards refer only to that worn by officers. There are also various orders of dress (q.v.) such as full dress, gala dress and undress.

Dress Regulations Although these may have been issued in separate instructions an attempt was made in 1802 to bring them all together. In 1811 a few meagre words were given in 'General Orders on Dress of Officers' and in 1816 a slightly larger edition of 16 pages on 'Dress of General and Staff Officers' appeared. The full Dress Regulations appeared in 1822 and were intended to be a guide (for tailors) as the officers had to provide their own uniforms. As other ranks were supplied officially with uniforms there was no reason for their regulations to be printed. In the 1860s a small series of books was published which was intended to cover the clothing and some equipment of the British Army but this did not continue. Dress Regulations for officers have appeared at intervals and official rulings are available today through the Stationery Office.

Drill jacket This garment intended for drill purposes has also been called over the many years a fatigue jacket, stable jacket or shell jacket. It was a very plain 'waistcoat' with sleeves. Although obsolete for most regiments about 1870 the white drill jacket was worn by the Foot Guards and Highland regiments up to the First World War and even past that time at tournaments and on display occasions.

Drillichjacke German drill jacket.

Driver (Horse transport) In August 1877 an arm badge was introduced for skilled drivers. The crossed whips and spur were embroidered in both gold and worsted. Later the highest category wore a crown as well. By the time of the First World War the badge was simplified to a single whip and spur. When the horse disappeared from the regular army so did the badge.

Driver (mechanical transport) An arm badge of a formalised steering wheel was introduced in 1925 to be worn on the left forearm. The 1st prize grading of the award also included an embroidered crown. Worn at first only by the Royal Army Service Corps, in 1927 the use was widened to include artillerymen. In wartime 'prizes' were discontinued but the badges were now worn for 'skill-at-arms'. About 1950 this badge was dis-

Driver. Proficiency badges, with star for 2nd class, *c.*1939

Duke of Edinburgh's Award. Arm badges embroidered for three categories

continued and the star (q.v.) worn by the Royal Tank Corps 1st class driver in 1936 became the trade badge for all drivers (q.v.).

Drum A badge of appointment going back at least as early as the first part of the 18th century. As drummers then wore cloth caps it was possible for them to have a drum embroidered on same. Later when the fur cap came in use a small badge of a drum was worn at the back, and this continued on later headdresses. The dress of the drummer was often enough to distinguish him from his fellow soldiers by his coat of facing colour. In 1831 drummers' coats were to be red and so a further distinction was needed. The arm badge of a drum made this distinction and it is worn to the present day in infantry regiments. The Foot Guards with their laced red coats do not need the badge.

Drum-major The original role of the drum-major had greater powers than those of today, covering not only the teaching of drumming but of recruitment and punishment. As drummers in an infantry regiment wore a special dress so did the drum-major but with the addition of silver lace (gold, of course, in the Foot Guards). The drum-major wore over his shoulder a broad sash which held a pair of token drumsticks, and later the regimental honours and distinctions. The elaborate mace or staff is said to have come from the shorter cane or stick originally used for punishment. In 1865 the badge worn by a drum-major was a drum over gold chevrons above the elbow. In 1881 when drum-majors were called sergeant-drummers four reversed chevrons were on the cuff. In 1928 the title of drum-major was restored but the same distinctions remained.

Drummers When the standing army was formed in the 17th century it was the fashion to dress drummer in 'reversed facings'. The normal soldier wore a red coat but the facings were often the choice of the colonel and perhaps part of his coat-of-arms. Thus drummers wore a kind of livery, the colour of the facings with extra lace as any groom or servant may have worn. But the collar, cuffs and linings were red. The seams and arms had special lace which eventually became the drummers' pattern of the regiment and lasted until 1872 when the 'crown' lace came in. In 1831 'reversed' facings were discontinued and the red coats of the drummer were now distinguished by the lace or braid. The red crown of 1872 was for all infantry of the line while the Foot Guards continued the blue fleur-de-lys (q.v.).

Duck Strong untwilled linen or cotton fabric used for trousers or fatigue suits. See also 'Ravenduck'.

Duke of Edinburgh's Award This award, which came into being in the late 1950s, has three divisions, badges for which are worn on the arm by the ACF, etc. There is the Bronze award, which is yellow silk on maroon, the Silver award, which is white silk on green and the Gold award, which is yellow silk on white.

Dummies These dummies, barrels or ornaments were worn at the back of short jackets about the beginning of the 19th century.

E A capital letter 'E' was used to denote proficiency in English worn by non-British troops. A black 'E' on red was worn on both shoulders in the Indian Army before the Second World War. Black on a green circle was worn by Africans and red on red by Malayans and Chinese.

An 'E' combined with two flashes of lightning is a badge worn by Equipment fitters in the Royal Artillery and REME.

EAG The Experimental Assistant Gunnery has a post-war arm badge which included the letters EAG and a theodolite within a laurel spray.

Eagle Many types of eagles are utilised in the British Army as badges. (a) The French Eagle, taken from the top of captured Napoleonic regimental colours, in badges of the Royal Dragoons (captured at Waterloo), Royal Scots Greys (captured at Waterloo), Royal Irish Fusiliers and the Essex Regiment (all today with different titles); (b) Prussian eagle. Worn by the 14th Light Dragoons because of the Duchess of York 1798 who was Princess Royal of Prussia and who gave her name to the regiment; (c) Austrian double-headed eagle granted to the King's Dragoon Guards when Emperor Francis Joseph of Austria became Colonel-in-Chief in 1896; (d) Airborne Eagle worn by the Army Air Corps and the Glider Pilot but with slight differences of position; (e) other varieties as worn by the Bedfordshire Yeomanry and the Lanarkshire Yeomanry; (f)the American eagle has served as a rank badge in the US Army. For the colonel this was in silver but before the First World War a general had a gold eagle between two silver stars, changed later to three stars only.

Many nations have the national eagle as part of the devices carried by their soldiers. (a) America has a single-headed eagle with a shield carrying the Stars and Stripes on its chest and some-times from the beak a scroll with 'E Pluribus Unum'. The claws may also carry arrows and foliage. The rank badge of a colonel is an eagle. (b) Austria had a two-headed eagle with a red and white shield on its chest but in modern times a single-headed eagle serves as a cap badge, etc. (c) France had the Roman eagle in the days of the first Napoleon. This stood on a thunderbolt and acquired a crown in the days of the Empire, although the crown disappeared in Republican years. The eagle appeared on headdress, buttons and elsewhere. (d) The Polish White Eagle had a crown when the country had a monarch but after the First World War this was discontinued. The eagle appears on headdress and buttons. (e) Prussia had the crowned eagle carrying in its claws the sceptre (or sword) and orb. This eagle appeared on helmets. (f) Russia in the time of the Czars had the double-headed eagle with varying

Eagle. Badge as worn by Essex Regiment

Elephant. Badge of 19th Queen Alexandra's Own Hussars, *c.1920*

coats-of-arms on the chest. Once again worn extensively on head-dress.

Ear boss These ornaments were above each ear on a headdress to make a fixing point for the chin-chain or chin-scales. Frequently a regimental device appeared in the centre like a grenade, bugle-horn, crown, etc.

Efficiency badge Awarded to the old volunteers, members of the Territorial Force, the Territorial Army, the Officers Training Corps and Army cadets. A ring of silver braid around the right cuff was the first efficiency mark for volunteers. There could also be a further award of a star or stars for every fourth efficient year. The braid was replaced by a hollow diamond, the stars still being worn. Eventually in Edward VII's reign stars only were worn.

Egret The feathery plumage of the Lesser White Heron was used in the headdress, particularly of 19th century hussars.

Elephant The animal is the badge of certain regiments who served in India, like the Duke of Wellington's Regiment and others. It was also an arm badge for NCOs in the 19th Hussars and the headdress distinction for the old 24th Light Dragoons and the war-raised 27th Lancers.

Eisenhower jacket Named after General Dwight D. Eisenhower who wore a short jacket apparently inspired by the British battle-dress blouse.

Embroidery Expert needlework frequently appeared on soldiers, especially officers', uniforms. Elaborately embroidered button-holes in gold or silver wire were made in the earliest days to strengthen the holes and continued in substance to modern time although lace or braid was more frequently worn. Gorget patches, undress cap badges and mess badges were all minor works in embroidery to be paid for by officers. Other ranks' distinctions which are embroidered like the elaborate ones worn by the Foot Guards are not paid for by the wearer unless lost.

The common soldier also had his personal embroidery in the first days of the army, for the grenadiers' cap was embroidered in coloured wools or silk, and in modern times not all arm badges are machine embroidered but some are hand-made. The senior NCOs of the Foot Guards have elaborate metal and silk embroidered arm badges for rank and appointment. For other units gold and silver embroidered badges appeared on blue or ceremonial uniforms and still appear although such embroidery is a dying art.

In the case of cavalry some of the finest examples of embroidery may be seen on the sabretaches and pouches which are much sought by collectors. Shabraques and housings of horses also had elaborate embroidery. Today such embroidery may be seen on regimental colours, standards and guidons as well as trumpet and drum banners. Other examples may be seen on the embroidered peaks of forage caps and the long-discontinued epaulettes are most intricate examples of the art; q.v. epaulettes, sabretache, etc.

Emsdorf This was the earliest battle honour to be worn by the

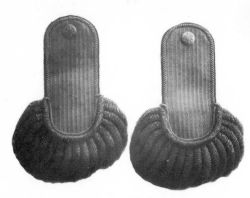

Epaulette. Officer, 42nd Highlanders, c.1820

Eyes. Cuff of officer's jacket, Royal Horse Artillery, c.1815

15th Light Dragoons in 1760 on their headdress after the battle of that name; q.v. 'battle honour'.

Ensign (a) The Royal badge on a colour was called an ensign (from Latin meaning insignia, a sign); (b) the officer who carried the flag or ensign of infantry in the 16th century was called an ensign. A colloquialism popular at that time was 'ancient' as quoted by Shakespeare but age seems to have little to do with the appointment. The title of ensign was changed to second (or sub) lieutenant in 1871 (q.v. 'rank badge').

Epaulette From the French, indicating a shoulder, for it was an ornamental piece of cloth and embroidery worn on the shoulder. Originating from a need to keep a shoulder sash or belt in position, the cords, ribbons or lace evolved into an elaborate fitment which at first indicated a regimental connection and later the rank of the officer. The cord or lace was in gold or silver depending on the regimental preference and the tied ends which hung over the point of the shoulder evolved into a fringe. The flattened ribbon or lace formed a strap which at first was soft and flexible. The fringe changed to bullion, hollow tubes of twisted wire, the quantity of which indicated the rank of the wearer. Then the strap was stiffened and given an edging of cord. The sequins and embroidery where the fringe or bullion joined the strap gave way to a metal plate of crescent shape. By 1830 the lower ends of the bullion were 'boxed', i.e. connected together and fixed so that it no longer hung loosely. Embroidered devices like the Prince of Wales' plume, thistles and crowns were adopted as regimental devices in the 18th century but by 1810 a system of crowns and stars indicated the officer's rank. These complicated ornaments were worn by the fighting officer up to 1855.

Epaulettes were also worn by other ranks. The light dragoons of the 1812 period wore either yellow or white epaulettes on both shoulders. Men of battalion companies of infantry and the Foot Guards wore epaulettes on the coatee which went out in the Crimean War. On the continent the epaulette was popular for most infantry especially in France where the Foreign Legion wore them until modern times.

Equerry An officer of the Royal Household who wears a uniform very similar to that of an ADC.

Equipment Although equipment may refer to the material of a regiment such as vehicles, guns, etc., the personal equipment of a soldier refers to the items worn with his uniform. This includes belts, pouch, knapsack, canteen etc. This varies much according to rank, appointment, unit and period. Strictly it is not uniform although without it a uniform would be incomplete.

Esquavar Nether wear of continental hussars, see 'charivara'.

Eyes, eyeing The small circular patterns made with tracing or cord so popular on uniform in the late 18th century. The complete circles formed a pattern around other braid or trimming on jackets and trousers of hussars and light cavalry, as well as horse artillery.

Facings This refers to the material used to face or partly line the soldier's coat from the 17th century onwards. When the long sleeves were turned back the resultant cuffs were of the 'facing' colour, as were the turned-back skirts, fronts and the collar. The red coat of the King's men would have Royal blue facings, the Queen or Catherine of Braganza her distinct sea-green. It was easy to recognise a regiment by its facings but as the number of regiments increased, there were not enough colours and so different patterns of lace and buttons brought further distinctions. In 1881 the facing colours of infantry were simplified to blue for Royal regiments, white for English and Welsh, yellow for Scottish and green for Irish. This was not, entirely popular and some regiments at once sought a change back to their regimental facings. The old 3rd Foot or Buffs at their own expense coloured their white facings buff and when this was officially allowed other regiments gradually received permission to change back. The outbreak of the First World War saw the end of men's full dress and further changes in facings. In modern times regimental colours may be found on blue uniforms, not as facings but as the pipings on shoulder-straps.

Farion The Greek word for the fez worn by the Evzones. This headdress is made of red felt and has a black tassel known as the 'founda'.

Farrier A farrier in the British Army wears the badge of a horseshoe (q.v.), and farrier sergeants wear it over their chevrons. The dress of a farrier attached to a cavalry regiment was distinctive even in the 18th century. He wore a blue coat so as not to show the dirt and his headdress was a fur cap. On the front plate of the cap it was usual to display the badge of a horseshoe. A leather apron was part of his dress and an axe was carried, even on horseback. The Household Cavalry farrier of today has somewhat similar distinctions but with the helmet. For cavalry of the line the special dress disappeared in the 19th century.

Fatigue dress A simple dress worn on non-militant duties. A long coat of grey wool was worn in the 18th century. Later a soldier would remove his coat and wear a cloth cap instead of a hat to perform menial duties. By the end of the century stout overalls were worn and a short jacket was also available usually in white or a light-coloured material. Red fatigue jackets were ordered for infantry in 1844 but the Foot Guards continued to wear white jackets up to the 20th century as did the Highlanders. Light cavalry men wore dark blue fatigue jackets. With the advent of khaki these fatigue garments went out of use although canvas suits and overalls took their place.

Farrier. Life Guards, *c.*1829

Fausthandschuhe German, mittens or fingerless gloves.

Faustriemen German, cavalry sword-knot or strap.

Feather The feather is worn by native warriors in their headdress as a sign that they have the spirit of an eagle, the speed of a bird or some other attribute. Thus Highlanders wore such a distinction before the regular army was formed. It would appear that the Black Watch when in America adopted black feathers for their caps, either ostrich or turkey (see also 'feather bonnet'). The hussar in his fur cap wore a feather following the custom of the Hungarian cavalryman. In the American Revolution many infantrymen took to wearing the local feathers cut as hackles or in plumes to distinguish themselves. The light dragoon helmet of 1783 acquired feathers at the side and even today fusiliers and guardsmen wear distinguishing feathers, thus continuing a fashion begun in the Ancient World.

Feather(ed) Bonnet The Highlanders' knitted bonnet acquired black feathers *c*.1763. As more and more feathers were added the original bonnet disappeared from view being hidden by curled pieces, tails and/or flats, often on a wire framework (see also 'dicing'). The various plumes worn by infantry companies on shakoes in the 19th century were adopted from the feather bonnet.

Fechtabzeichen German, distinctions for proficiency in arms.

Feder-busch German, the impressive ornament made of feathers worn in front of the shako in the 19th century.

Federn German, feathers.

Feile-beg, feilidh-beag, etc. Gaelic, little kilt, not the full plaid (feile mor).

Feile-mor Gaelic, full belted plaid (q.v.).

Feldbinde German, waist-belt, scarf or sash usually of metallic lace.

Feld grau German, field grey, the service colour for German uniform introduced by AKO 23 February 1910 although it had been tried earlier.

Feather(ed) Bonnet. Highlanders in Paris, 1815

Field cap. 1st Bucks Rifle Volunteers, buttons at both ends

Feldkappe German, undress cap in Austrian Army near end of 19th century.

Feldmütze German, an undress cap in use as early as 1808 but continued in wear with minor variations until the 20th century.

Fencibles Fencible (defensive) troops were introduced into the British Army in the 18th century intended to be limited to the defence of Great Britain. Intended to serve in time of war only but there were exceptions like the Royal Malta Fencibles who continued throughout the 19th century. The fencibles from 1794 onwards wore the normal infantry (or Scottish) uniform for the foot soldiers and the cavalry were dressed as the light cavalry with variously coloured jackets, and the leather helmets.

Fermeli Greek, the waistcoat worn by the mountain soldiers, the Evzones.

Fernglas German, telescope.

Ferreting Stout cotton or silk tape used to edge or decorate uniforms.

Ferrule The lower end of a sword scabbard or pace stick.

Festoon The elaborate plaited cord on the front of some shakoes which usually finished in two cords and tassels which were fixed to the body to prevent the headdress being lost.

Fez The red cap worn by Turkish and Zouave troops. Also under the turban of West Indian troops.

Field cap A cap for use in the field, normally of soft material. The folding cap introduced in 1883 was for 'active service or peace manoeuvres'. In 1888 the new pattern field service cap (also flat and folding) was approved for all troops with round forage caps but not taken into general use until 1894. In 1896 the infantry glengarry (except for Scottish regiments) was replaced by a folding cap with two buttons in front. The 'cap.f.s. coloured' was re-introduced as an optional item in 1937. These by no means exhaust the variations.

Field dressing The first field dressing was introduced in the Crimean War. It consisted of a calico bandage, lint and pins. Originally carried in the knapsack it was by 1874 carried in the left breast pocket of the tunic. In 1884 antiseptic first field dressings were issued. Various changes in the components of the dressing took place but it became part of the soldier's uniform on active service, inside the tunic in the First World War and in the right-hand front pocket of battledress trousers in the Second World War (at the back for parachutists).

Field glasses 'Spy' glasses, to espy (discern) the enemy, were in use in the 17th century. By the second half of the 19th century a special pouch to carry a pair of glasses or binoculars was on the shoulder-belt of Royal Engineer officers in full dress. Staff officers also had these cases until King Edward VII's reign. Later the heavy cases were only for active service or simulated conditions.

Field Mark In the 17th century soldiers' dress was so similar to opposing forces that a field mark and/or field word was necessary

Flag. Embroidered blue and white signalling flags for arm badge

Flap. Officer, Coldstream Guards with 'economy' lace

during battle. Scottish troops had long worn a clan distinction in the headdress like heather or other floral devices. Green leaves or the local vegetation could also be pressed into service. A piece of white paper in the hat, a handkerchief or even the wearing of the shirt tail outside the trousers all made the dress different from the enemy, although he might adopt the enemy's temporary mark to avoid capture.

Field security Those infantry soldiers who were trained for field security wore the letters 'FS' embroidered within a spray of laurels on the forearm. The initials 'FS' were also to be seen on the armlet of the Field Security Police in the Second World War.

Field Service Cap A pattern introduced in 1888 (q.v. 'Field cap').

Fifer With a drummer he formed the 'music' for a company in the 16th century up to the 20th. Fifes were not considered proper instruments in the Cromwellian army but came back in strength with the Restoration of the monarchy. The dress in the earliest days was as that of a drummer. The Foot Guards had the red coat (as up to the present day) and the infantry had the 'reversed facing' coat. Fifes, in the 18th century, were carried in long brass tubular cases hanging from coloured strings. Later, small leather pouches or cases were worn instead. When the companies were assembled the drummers and fifers could play together as a band. There was only an arm badge of a drum because drummers were expected to play the fife as well.

First field dressing The 'first aid' dressing to be used on the battlefield, see also 'field dressing'.

Fish tail (a) The black ribbon on the back of Highland headdress was sometimes cut with a 'V'-shaped notch which was called a fish tail; (b) Garter flashes, colourful ornaments worn under the turned-downs of hose and hose-tops in tropical dress, usually have fish-tail ends.

Flag The infantry flags are known as 'colours' but those on a colour-sergeant's (or recruiter's) arm badge are sometimes called flags. The arm badge of men qualified in hand-signalling has two crossed signalling flags normally embroidered in white and blue.

Flamme French, referring to the loose end on hussars' caps – both the mirliton and the busby.

Flank companies The addition, in the 18th century, of a grenadier company on the right and later a light infantry company on the left to the centre companies of an infantry battalion led to the description 'flank' companies. The grenadier company usually had the special cap of cloth or fur and the light company their own version of headdress. Later coloured plumes or balls marked the distinctions. Both flank companies wore wings on their shoulders. Flank companies were discontinued soon after the Crimean War.

Flap (a) To keep the turn-back of the sleeve in position in the 18th century a buttoned flap was added. This flap later developed into the three-pointed flap on the tunic which is still worn today

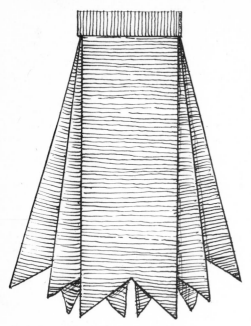

Flash. Worn at back of collar by Royal Welsh Fusiliers

by the Guardsman with three or more buttons; (b) the cartridge pouch of the 18th century had a leather flap going over the top and down the front to keep the ammunition dry. A badge in brass was placed on this flap as an ornament although it was claimed that its weight kept the flap down (q.v. 'pouch ornament').

Flash (a) The ribbon to tie the queue (q.v.) at the end of the 18th century was sometimes called the flash. When queues were abolished *c.*1808 the Royal Welsh Fusiliers were abroad and continued to wear their ribbon or flash. It continued to be worn in the following centuries as a fixed ornament sewn at the back of the collar; (b) the cloth signs introduced in the First World War and worn on the arms were sometimes called flashes; (c) the ribbon or tape end which appear from the turn-down of hose in Highland and tropical dress is also known as a garter-flash (q.v. 'fish-tail').

Flaskcord The cord used to hold the powder flask of cavalry went over the shoulder and was perpetuated by heavy cavalry, regiments of horse. The Royal Horse Guards continued to wear the flaskcord in the 19th century even though the purpose had gone and in 1829 the Life Guards also adopted the custom. Some yeomanry regiments also wore the flaskcord on the belt, the Bedfordshire being one.

Flats The flat and uncurled feathers worn on the Highland bonnet in the 19th century were known as flats.

Fleur-de-lys Besides being the badge of the Manchester Regiment, the fleur-de-lys is the device in the drummer's lace of the Foot Guards. This blue flower demonstrated that France was part of the British royal coat-of-arms up to 1801.

Flounders This term applies to the interlaced and plaited knots on the cap- (or shako-) lines of the 18th century. In France the term 'raquettes' is used.

Flügelman Obviously taken from the German, this man on the wing of the company was expected to advance and demonstrate drill movements for the benefit of the other soldiers. He did not wear any special distinction for this task.

Flügelmutze German, 'winged cap', the cylindrical cap of light cavalry with the piece of cloth flying loosely like a wing.

Flying badge Certain officers and men in the British Army may qualify for a flying badge – the Army Air Corps, the Glider Pilot Regiment (now disbanded) and Air landing units as well as air observation staff. The pilot wears on his left breast the embroidered badge of the winged Royal Crest. The Second Glider Pilot has 'G' on a winged disk. The Air Observation Post Pilot working with the artillery has a grenade with wings. Other badges include that of the observer with a crowned 'O' and a single wing, and the air gunner with a crowned 'G' and a single wing. The Parachute Regiment which was part of the Army Air Corps in 1942 became an infantry corps in 1949.

Fly plaid This is the name given to the piece of tartan attached at the shoulder in Highland dress. As it flies loose at the lower end

Fleur-de-lys. Drummer's lace on shoulder-strap of Coldstream Guards

Formation sign. Embroidered, 1st Army, Second World War

it is so named.

Foot Guards Being the 'King's men' these soldiers from the 17th century wore the Royal livery of red and blue. By 1774 the system of distinguishing the three regiments by buttons arranged regularly, in pairs or in threes had begun. When the Irish Guards were formed in 1900 they had their buttons in fours and the Welsh Guards of 1915 had theirs in fives. The plumes in the fur cap are also individual. The Grenadier Guards had a white plume on the left as proper for grenadiers. In 1831 the Coldstream Guards wore a red plume on the right, which they still do. The Scots Guards, when given the fur cap for all, had the white plume on the left but discontinued it in 1838. The Irish Guards had a plume of St Patrick's blue on the right and the Welsh Guards have white, green and white on the left.

Foot Guards drummers These men do not wear coats of the facing colour but the red of the sovereign with the royal blue facings. The sleeves with lace or braid in chevrons follows very early dress. The lace in the 18th century had been royal lace of red blue and yellow but it changed to white with a fleur-de-lys pattern worn today (q.v. 'fleur-de-lys').

Footwear This obviously followed civilian styles in the early days but in modern times has become specialised (see also 'Boot'). Infantry for many years wore the shoe before adopting a boot in 1823. Highland regiments wore shoes for many years later, specially in the case of pipers and for undress use. See also brogues, currans, George boot, moccasin and sandals.

Forage cap Originally a cap smaller than the normal headdress worn by cavalrymen when collecting forage for the horse. Later applied to the undress caps generally worn by cavalrymen when the full dress headdress was to be preserved and not worn. Frequently round and stiffened with or without a peak, in the case of men. In infantry regiments officers wore peaks. In 1898 a broad topped peaked cap based on the naval pattern was experimentally introduced and this was called a forage cap, as it is today.

Fore-and-aft This nautical term is applied to the bicorn hat which, at the beginning of the 19th century, was worn with the corners pointing forwards and backwards instead of across the shoulders.

Formation sign Because of the need for security in the First World War, many vehicles were painted with symbols and markings only known to the Allies. This idea was extended to the soldiers who were given cloth patches for their uniform. These cloth signs had been worn before in the American Civil War but in the 20th century spread to most fighting nations. Armies, corps, divisions, brigades, regiments, battalions and even companies may wear their own distinctive sign. The subject is obviously too vast to cover here.

Foul-weather cap The caps introduced in the 19th century were lightweight versions of the military headdresses which in bad

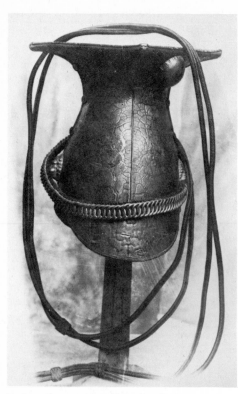

Foul-weather cap. Lance cap and cords, *c.*1850

weather were covered with heavy waterproof oilcloth. The foul-weather cap was mainly of paste-board with a thin waterproof cover simulating both shako and lance cap.

Founda The Greek name given to the black tassel on the Evzone's fez.

Foundez The leg tassels tied over the stockings of the Evzone, just below the knee.

Fouraschka Russian field cap.

Fourragères French, shoulder-knots, worn as honour awards.

Foxtail (a) The cravats (q.v.) especially those worn by grenadiers in the late 17th century had foxtail ends (indented) possibly serrated; (b) certain long feathers on the Highland feather bonnet were known as foxtails.

Frac French, a long-tailed coat.

Fringes Fringe has appeared on military uniforms for a variety of reasons. (a) The scarf worn by officers and sergeants had fringe from the very beginning but now remains only at the lower end of the tie. Fringe was also on the baldrics or cloth sword-belts, a relic of this is to be seen on the sashes or belts worn by drum-majors; (b) the fringe end of the shoulder knot was followed by the fringe on an epaulette. Although bullion wire replaced the thin fringe of officers in the 19th century, other ranks' epaulettes and wings retained their fabric fringe; (c) gloves at the end of the 17th century had fringe around the 'gauntlet' cuff; (d) light cavalry had fringe on their jackets at the end of the 18th century, usually around the front braiding or looping. When the light dragoon jacket of 1812 was introduced there was a fringe in the small of the back (see 'Wasserfal', 'waterfall') a fashion which continued a few years later when lancers were introduced into the British Army.

Frock Originally a long-skirted loose coat but it evolved in two directions. A long coat is worn by officers of the Foot Guards in undress and some bandmasters also wear a long double-breasted blue coat. General officers also have a long blue coat introduced in the 19th century.

The other version is the serge frock which is cut like a tunic, but being looser and lighter in weight was worn as a type of undress coat in India and warm climates. It could be either red or blue, or even in dark green or black.

Frock coat The long frock as quoted above.

Frog (a) The attachment to a belt for a bayonet or a sword; (b) a coat fastening of braid or cord to go over a button, olivet, or toggle. Worn by hussars and others on certain undress coats (see 'Brandenburg').

Frogdrop loop An ornamental loop embroidered in gold or silver wire on early 19th century coats of certain military staff inspired by the frog of light cavalry.

Frogging The ornamental looping for fastening a coat or jacket made up of frogs (q.v.).

FS Initials on the Field Security (q.v.) arm badge.

Frock Coat. Officer, 5th Dragoon Guards, *c*.1860

Full dress The uniform worn on ceremonial occasions is the full dress as all the elaborate headdresses, embroidered pouches and special sashes are to be seen. The levee or galadress includes most full dress items but may be modified by special overalls or trousers and frequently cocked hats (*chapeaux de bras*).

Furbelows The trimmings on hunting shirts and trousers at the time of the American Revolution were known as furbelows, being the fringe sometimes of linen or woollen.

Furniture In the military connotation does not mean 'table and chairs' but that which is furnished. In the case of a soldier, that which is added to his clothing and in the case of a horse, the equipment, especially the shabraque, holster-caps, sheepskin and suchlike.

Fusilier The fusil was the firearm with a flintlock. When introduced to replace the matchlock its expense allowed it only to be issued to certain regiments. These included the Royal Fusiliers (who guarded the artillery) the Royal Scots Fusiliers and the Royal Welch Fusiliers. As the fusil had slings and could be slung over the shoulder to leave the hands free, a cloth cap instead of the large hat was allowed. The cloth cap changed in the 18th century to a fur cap, slightly smaller than that of grenadiers. Although later all infantry regiments received flintlocks, only the original regiments retained the title (certain other regiments were named fusiliers as an honour). In Europe some nations called their normal infantry regiments fusiliers. British fusiliers carry the flaming grenade badge, as do grenadier companies.

Fustanella Greek, for the many pleated kilt of the evzone.

Fuzee Normally the light flintlock carried by officers in the 18th century but sometimes wrongly applied to the flaming grenade badge.

G

Gaiter-trousers. Light company man, Foot Guards, c1794

G This letter with laurels formed the arm badge for those artillery men qualified for a prize badge or a skill-at-arms badge for gunnery. There were three grades, the lowest described as the 3rd prize, with a star above for the 2nd prize and with a crown above for the 1st prize.

Gaberdine A strong diagonally woven cloth in wool or cotton. Popular for officers' khaki service dress tunics in the early part of the 20th century.

Gaiters These cloth items were introduced at the end of the 17th century to protect the soldiers' hose and also to prevent dirt and mud getting into the low-cut shoes. They buttoned down the outside of the leg and they usually had a garter strap just below the knee. The gaiter top came just above the knee. Later it was stiffened. The strap under the instep also buckled at the outside of the leg although the buckle was not always employed. Gaiters were usually white or grey but by 1760 black was chosen as the working colour. White gaiters continued to be worn for full dress in the 19th century, 1823 being the last year for infantry of the line. In 1771 the new light infantry wore short black gaiters as high as the calf behind. In the Napoleonic wars the gaiters were grey or black worn with trousers. Highlanders continued to wear their spats until modern times.

Gaiter, leather In 1862 short leather gaiters were introduced for line infantry men. These continued in use for the rest of the century being replaced eventually by puttees. Just before the Second World War, canvas gaiters were tried experimentally and continued to be worn with the battle dress in action.

Gaiter trousers (gaiter-trowsers) In 1791 gaiter-trousers were worn over breeches in order to protect them. These were one-piece nether garments made fitting tight to the calf and buttoned on the outside of the leg. They were of white cloth and are shown later in pictures of the Foot Guards and volunteers. Obviously as they were lightweight they were popular in the East and Indian troops frequently appear in them according to contemporary pictures.

Gala anzug German, the gala walking-out dress for special non-drill occasions.

Gala dress A variation of full dress worn on gala occasions like the levees at St James's Palace or other royal occasions.

Galawoch anzug Duty dress on gala occasions.

Galloon, Galon Braid for wearing on coats and hats in the 17th century. Could be gold or silver silk or cotton, not a rich metal.

Gamaschen German, gaiters.

Gant-à-crispin French, short gloves worn in Napoleonic times

Garter flashes. Royal Signals and Royal Army Service Corps.

(no gauntlet cuff).

Garibaldi shirt The successful irregular troops under Garibaldi often wore red shirts, a fashion that was later copied by volunteers in Great Britain and in America.

Garter The early gaiters (q.v.) needed a garter just below the knee to keep them up. The garters were buckled and either of leather or stout cloth. Officially gaiters and garter disappeared *c*.1823 when trousers were introduced for general wear instead of breeches. The drum-majors of the Foot Guards in full dress still wear white gaiters and garters.

Garter, Order of the This Order frequently appears in badges and on the soldier's dress. The Garter is a depicted in a circle with the end hanging down on such badges as the Royal Fusiliers which has a Rose in the centre. It should have the motto HONI SOIT QUI MAL Y PENSE. If there is other lettering then it is not a true garter but a strap.

Garter-flash See also 'flash'. Although Highlanders originally kept their hose in place with a ribbon or tape of red material, it became the fashion for other troops in hot climates to adopt the 'garter' with tropical hose-tops. In this case the tops were held up with tapes or some other material and the ornamental ends were added to hang down as flashes. These were (and are) in regimental or corps colours with fancy cut ends.

Garter Star The star of the Order of the Garter has been used as a regimental badge and as a badge of rank, in the Foot Guards – that is to say in the Grenadier Guards, the Coldstream Guards and Welsh Guards but not the Scots Guards who have the star of the Order of the Thistle, and the Irish Guards who have the star of the Order of St Patrick.

Gas mask A device introduced in 1915 when gas attacks started. At first a primitive cloth affair (impregnated at the time), it developed to include eye protections and a purifying container (see also 'respirator').

Gauntlets Gauntlets were part of a knight's armour but the name continued in use for the leather gloves with a 'gauntlet' cuff, worn by cavalrymen. These stout gloves continued in use until the last days of full dress.

GC General Officer. Above regimental officers were staff officers who did not necessarily command regiments but were concerned with the administration of troops. Above them are the general officers who are responsible for the conduct of war and include such ranks as major-general, lieutenant-general, general and field marshal. There are also certain equivalent officers in non-fighting services like surgeon-major-general. The basic rank distinction for generals is the badge with crossed sword and baton whereas the field marshal has crossed batons. The full dress uniform of the 18th century was red with blue facings and gold lace and buttons, the latter being arranged in twos, threes and regularly from the junior general upwards. In the 19th century the ivory-hilted Mameluke

Geneva Cross. Arm badge with silver for volunteers, c.1890

sword with simple cross quillons was introduced as their distinctive arm.

General service pattern button In the hopes of simplifying the number of regimental buttons, a general service pattern was introduced in 1871. This had the Royal Arms and was intended for other ranks being both in brass and white metal. It was of value in time of war when secrecy as to a unit was necessary.

Geneva cross When the Swiss introduced new humanitarian laws to the battlefield in 1864, the reversed colours of the Swiss national flag (red cross on white instead of white cross on red) served as the mark of a non-combatant who was to be protected. This Geneva Cross was worn on the arm of qualified Medical Corps personnel (not officers). In the regular army the circular device was edged with gold for NCOs and yellow thread for others. In the volunteers silver or white borders were worn. Although worn on khaki uniform up to the First World War, it is no longer a uniform distinction.

George boot A new light pattern boot was approved in November 1951 to be worn by officers in No. 1 and No. 3 dress. It was called the George boot and was slightly higher than a shoe but not as high as the common boot.

Gesellschaft anzug German, walking-out or society dress for evening wear.

Gibraltar An early battle honour to be granted to British and Allied troops in the Siege of Gibraltar which lasted from 1779 to 1783. The name was allowed to be carried on 'appointments' (q.v.) beltplates, drums, fronts of grenadier caps. The descendants of the Hanoverian regiments which were present at the siege wore a light blue armband with GIBRALTAR up to the First World War.

Gilding metal The metal used for badges (copper and tin) was a basic mixture suitable to take a gilt finish. But often 'ungilt' badges were worn.

Gilt many metal fittings of officer quality are given a thin gold covering, i.e. gilt. Other ranks' metal would be brass, gilding metal or possibly bronze. Senior NCOs may have their badges gilded.

Gimpe (also *besatzschnur*) German, narrow braid worn on shakos.

Girdle A type of waistbelt usually worn by light cavalry. The hussar sash (q.v.) could be considered such an item, but that worn

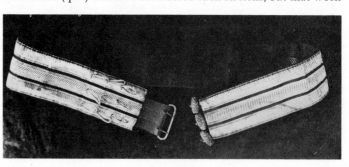

Girdle. Lancer type with olivets and loops

64

by lancers and light dragoons is more typical. This woven waist-sash is often mounted on leather or given a stiffened back. Officers might wear the girdle in gold or silver wire with coloured stripes running horizontally. The fastening by toggles, olivets or a type of button going through cord loops, in the British Army is on the left side. Other ranks have cloth girdles. The light dragoon of 1812 had stripes of the facing colour combined with white or yellow to match the officer's metal lace.

Glengarry This Scottish headdress is based on the blue woollen bonnet, which is folded flat but retains a small red tourie at the top and keeping the black ribbon ends at the back. It is said that the first recorded military use is that of a piper of the 74th Foot. Earlier pictures of civilians and fencible infantry may show the glengarry or another version of a folded bonnet. Highland regiments wore this cap for undress but in 1868 it was introduced for all infantry regiments including English. Although discontinued for some in 1890, Scottish regiments continued its use to the present day. Dicing (q.v.) is not always worn and patterns of this vary. Even the red tuft is not universal for the London Scottish have a Royal blue tuft and black tufts were worn by riflemen like the Cameronians.

Gloves Gloves have been worn from the earliest days to protect the soldier's hand from harm by weapons, including their own. Officers in the late 17th century found gloves useful when the enveloping hand guard could chafe. Pikemen with long unwieldy pikes wore gloves to avoid splinters. Cavalrymen found stout leather gauntlets a safeguard with reins and as a protection against sword cuts.

In the 18th century officers gloves were known to have been ornamented with regimental devices. Gloves for parade purposes in the 19th century were elegant with rifle officers wearing black, leather for officers and woollen for men. In the 20th century warfare made khaki gloves a necessity and the introduction of the motor cycle brought about a stout leather gauntlet. Gloves are also permitted in modern times for all soldiers when walking out.

G/M Abbreviation for gilding metal (q.v.) for badges and fittings.

Goatskin This relatively inexpensive animal skin was used for knapsacks in the 18th century with the long hair still left on. It was also used for horse furniture as well as strips on horseclothes of certain light dragoons in the 18th century. Goatskin has also been used for the white fur cap of the kettledrummer of the Royal Scots Greys.

Goggles (a) Troops serving in the Egyptian campaign (1882) and the Sudan campaign were given 'sand goggles' or sand-glasses as a protection against the sudden sand storms; (b) goggles were found to be necessary for motor-cyclists in the First World War. The early perishable patterns underwent many changes until the improved version of today, not only for temperate climates but also for vehicle drivers and desert areas.

Gorget. Gilt universal pattern introduced in 1796

Gold Stick The carrying of a gold stick or a silver stick is said to have originated with a conspiracy of 1528 when King Henry VIII appointed officers to guard him closely. In 1678 these titles were granted to officers of the King's Guards and still apply today to officers not only of the Life Guards and the Royal Horse Guards but to the Gentlemen-at-Arms and the Royal Company of Archers. Apart from the carrying of the gold or silver stick there is no addition to the holder's uniform.

Good conduct awards Chevrons were introduced in the French army in 1777 to indicate long service as well as good conduct. In the British Army it was not until 1836 that chevrons were to be worn on the right forearm for this distinction. In 1881 the chevrons were moved to the left forearm with the points upwards, one for two years, two for six years and so on. Although they are worn point upwards in most cases, when they are worn on the time-beater's or drummer's tunic in the Foot Guards they are worn point downwards so as not to be confused with the drummer's ornamental chevrons.

Gorget The gorget worn by British Army officers from 1660 to 1830 originated as a piece of a knight's suit of armour. The name 'gorget' came from the French *gorge* meaning throat. The armour was originally in two pieces, front and back, to take the weight of the cuirass, and the last to be taken off. The front piece remained in service as a reminder that signified the high status of the wearer. It was worn as a 'duty' sign and in the 18th century was either of silver or silver-gilt to match the metal of the buttons. The army officers were expected to have the Royal Arms on the gorget. In 1796 all gorgets were to be gilt and to carry the Royal Cypher which remained in use until 1830. The size was gradually reduced until the final pattern measured about three inches by four. A ribbon (or ribbons) was used to suspend the gorget from the neck.

Gorget patches In the 19th century the gorget was frequently suspended by means of ribbon to the buttons on either side of the collar. These buttons were often on a patch of colour or gold or silver lace or embroidery.

Towards the end of the 19th century when distinctions were needed for the new khaki uniform, colour patches were placed on the collar. Scarlet being chosen to indicate general and staff officers. Other colours were later chosen, like the blue for supply and the green for training. In 1940 miniature gorget patches were introduced for service dress, battle dress, etc. Brigadiers had coloured braid loops to the button but general officers and field marshals had gold gimp or gold embroidery.

Gorgon's head The horrific head of gorgon was said to terrify the enemy in ancient times and often appeared on a shield. Thus the use of a gorgon's head on the front of light dragoon helmets in the 18th century was not unexpected. At the end of the century it appeared on the 'tin' helmets worn by cavalry in the East. Later in the 19th century a small metal ornament of the gorgon's head

Gorget patches. Gold embroidered for general officers, red braid for colonels

served to cover the ventilator of officers' shakos.

Graugrün Grey-green was the colour of the uniform of the German *jägers* and machine gun corps. Later adopted for other German soldiers.

Greatcoat The terms 'greatcoat' and 'overcoat' are interchangeable. Originally the red coat was considered sufficient for the British infantryman although 'centinel coats' or watch coats were in limited supply for night duty. It was in 1801 that there was to be an issue of greatcoats of kersey weave, pepper and salt thick cloth. In 1803 sergeants were given collars and cuffs of the regimental facing colour. The grey coat of varying shades continued in use until the drab (khaki) greatcoat was introduced at the end of the 19th century. See also 'centinel coat' etc.

Grenade The badge of flaming grenade is worn by grenadiers, fusiliers, artillerymen and engineers. As a badge it was worn on the early cloth cap of grenadiers and it is still worn today as a cap badge of the Grenadier Guards and fusilier regiments. It was also worn on the belt-plate, pouch, shoulders, coat-tails and collars to distinguish grenadier companies or a fusilier regiment. Certain NCOs in the Royal Engineers wear a grenade over the rank badge. The Royal Scots Greys carrying on their tradition of mounted horse grenadiers also wore the grenade badge. In the First World War when the use of hand-grenades was re-introduced, it became the arm badge of the 'bomber' or grenade-thrower. An all-blue grenade was the badge for the mortar-bomber, buff with red

Grenade. Worn on arm in Grenadier Guards

Grenadier cap. Officer, Buffs, *c.*1760

flames for the battalion bomber and khaki and buff for the officer-instructor.

Grenadier A grenadier besides wearing the badge of a grenade on his cap, in the 18th century wore wings on his shoulders (see flank companies) but these were discontinued about the time of the Crimean War, when the flank companies were abandoned. The use of the grenade was very intermittent by the middle of the 18th century although they were issued on demand.

Grenadier cap Because the grenadier had to sling his firearm over his back to throw his grenade, the broad-brimmed hat was changed for the smaller grenadier cap, usually of cloth but sometimes fur-edged. A change of fashion in 1765 brought the all-fur cap to the British Army. The introduction of the shako in the 19th century brought about a gradual disuse of the fur cap of grenadier companies, especially on service. The introduction of the Albert shako saw its end except for fusiliers. The Foot Guards and the Royal Scots Greys continued to wear the fur cap but it was no longer called a grenadier cap.

Greyback The name given to the grey shirt worn by infantrymen in the 19th century.

Grey uniform Apart from grey greatcoats or overcoats, grey clothing was worn in the 18th century by *jägers*, some emigré units in British Army service. Grey uniforms were popular in the United States at the beginning of the 19th century and the West Point Cadets still wear it. Some militia units in Canada in the 1820s were given grey jackets and trousers as were three British light infantry regiments who were ordered to Canada in 1835. No doubt grey served as an early kind of camouflage but the British volunteers of 1859–60 frequently wore uniforms of grey because they paid for these themselves and grey was easily obtained. A shade of grey was produced for the British regular troops proceeding to Egypt in 1885. On the Continent pike-grey was popular in Austria, steel-grey in Finland and of course the field-grey in Germany.

Guards Royal guards, body guards and life guards usually have a more elaborate uniform than the common soldier and as such still exist for ceremonial purposes, even in communist countries. The variations of uniform are too many to cover here.

Guards' star Many Royal guards wore a badge based on the star of a Royal Order. The British Foot Guards have the Star of the Garter, the Thistle and St Patrick. Prussian Guards had the star of the Order of the Eagle, on their headdress.

Ground-sheet, cape This popular item of equipment issued in the Second World War was a rubberised fabric sheet which could act as a cape in wet weather or a ground-sheet on which to sleep. It was roughly rectangular in shape with a place for the neck in the middle of one of the long sides and with five bone buttons for fastening in front. Later, non-rubber sheets were introduced.

Guides Napoleon formed several corps of guides. Both Kent and

Grenadier. *c.*1778,

Sussex raised a corps of guides to help the populace in case of invasion by Napoleon but they were disbanded without action. On the Continent the use of guides continued in France, Belgium and Switzerland after peace had been declared. A dark green uniform was often the distinctive colour of their uniform. A much-later Canadian Corps of Guides had green facings to their khaki uniform. The British Army did not raise a corps of guides but a volunteer body, the Legion of Frontiersmen came into being after the Boer War with the aim of being guides in time of conflict, but they were never employed as such.

Guidon The guidon was a cavalry flag said to have originated in the term *guide homme*, a guide. The cavalry officer carrying the guidon was also called a guidon but this term was not generally used in the British Army. In 1674 the troops of Horse Guards were given a second cornet or guidon, which in 1679 was noted as ranking with a colonel. But the term was discontinued a few years later. There were no special distinctions for this rank.

Gum cloth An American term for a water-proofed sheet.

Gun-barrels A badge of crossed gun-barrels is worn by the Assistant Instructor of Gunnery, RA (q.v. AIG) and also worn as a skill-at-arms badge by NCOs who pass the Gunnery Staff course as authorised in the Maritime Regiment RA in the Second World War. They also marked battery and company prize winners from 1877 to 1921.

Gunnery Those proficient in gunnery have various arm badges, like the 'G' in laurels, 'L' for layer, etc., q.v. under 'title'.

Gymnasterka Russian, a military blouse with standing collar buttoning at the side. Worn outside trousers with a waistbelt.

Guards Star. Valise badge of Coldstream Guards

Hackle. Cut-feather hackle worn by Royal Regiment of Fusiliers

Hammer and pincers. Embroidered arm badge, white on khaki.

H Badge for anti-aircraft artillerymen qualified as 1st class height takers introduced in 1939. The men calculated the height of the attacking aircraft.

Haar-busch German, for the hair plume on headdress.

Habit veste French, type of coat favoured by Napoleon and worn by many of his troops. Closed at the chest but opening above the waist to reveal the waistcoat.

Hackle Short cut feathers made into a small bush or bound into a long plume. Popular with Scottish troops since the 18th century but also worn on the beret of infantry and on earlier headdresses.

Hair powder In the 18th century powder was popular for making the soldier's hair white, cheap flour being used on occasion. In warfare it was not used but it remained in vogue for officers in full dress until 1808.

Halberd, halbert A long-staffed weapon with a cutting and axelike head. Guards of halbardiers from the 16th century dwindled until the halberd remained as the weapon of sergeants. It continued as such until 1792 when it was replaced by the spontoon (q.v.), a pointed weapon with a cross-piece.

Halb stiefel German, short boot, usually laced, introduced for German infantry in 1819.

Half-gaiters In the early 18th century gaiters reached to the knees. When light infantry were formed later they favoured the short gaiter which only reached to the calf. When trousers were introduced half-gaiters (short gaiters or spats) were worn beneath them especially on active service. At the beginning of the 19th century Highlanders were wearing half gaiters over their hose and shoes. They are still worn in some Scottish regiments.

Half-pike Officers of pikemen in the early 16th century carried the whole pike like other pikemen. A warrant of 10 December 1695 stated that ensigns of foot and dragoons were to carry a half-pike, obviously a more manageable length. The king's order of 14 September 1743 (quoted in T. Symes *Military Guide*) stated that officers of foot were to have spontoons instead of half-pikes.

Half-star The proficiency badge of 'Cert. A' part one (for ACF) was the top half of the star granted for both parts I and II. It became obsolete in 1974 when a new system of stars was introduced.

Halsbinde German, cravat or neckcloth.

Hammer-hatchet A tool carried by early greandiers which had a hammer-head. It was to be used in clearing the way for the troops in an assault or attack.

Hammer and pincers This trade badge was in use before 1865 to signify an artificer in the artillery or engineers. It is still in use and widened to cover many trades, including fitters, mechanics, tool-makers, plumbers, panel-beaters, welders and such like.

Handschuhe German, gloves.

Hanging sleeves The medieval hanging sleeves of the doublet were worn in Tudor times as a livery dress and then by the drummers and fifers of an infantry regiment, or a trumpeter of cavalry. Thus musicians at the Restoration continued to wear the hanging sleeves, now reduced to a vestige and having no practical use. The gold-laced State Dress of Household Cavalry musicians still continue the old tradition with two narrow strips hanging from the shoulders and looped in the waistbelt. For infantry drummers and fifers the 'hanging sleeves' were discontinued by a Royal Warrant of 1768.

Hardee hat When the 1st and 2nd Cavalry Regiments were raised in America in 1855, they were given a provisional issue of felt hats instead of caps or shakos. Major William J. Hardee of the 2nd Cavalry is said to have been responsible for the introduction of these hats, inspired by the Kossuth hat.

Harp Being the badge chosen by Henry VII for Ireland, the harp appears frequently in Irish regimental badges. But it also appears as a musical symbol as on the embroidered arm badge worn by bandsmen after 1871 when it appeared in conjunction with two trumpets. The lyre badge replaced it.

Hat A head-covering with a brim all round the central crown. May be in felt, leather or other material. The high-crowned hat of Charles II's reign could be ornamented with ribbons and/or feathers. As the brim tended to 'flop' in wet weather, one side was frequently rolled or turned up in the late 17th century. In the next century it was turned up on all three sides, held in place with stays and a cockade (q.v.). At the end of the 18th century the infantry-men wore a cap or a shako but the officers retained the hat (now shaped as a bicorn) for state and ceremonial occasions. General officers and most 'civil' departmental officers continued to wear the cocked hat until the abolition of full dress. See also bicorn, tricorn, fore-and-aft etc.

Hatchet (or axe) Apart from practical use, crossed hatchets (q.v.) were worn as a badge for pioneers (q.v.).

Havelock In the American Civil War 'havelocks' (named after the British general, Sir Henry Havelock) were a light cloth covering with a neck curtain to be worn on headdresses. They had a short life in the field.

Havresac, haversack From the German, *haver, hafer* being 'oats' and 'sack'. Used to carry food for the soldier.

Hecht grau German, pike-grey, the colour of certain Austrian uniforms.

Helm German for helmet.

Helmadler German, the metal eagle on the plate in front of helmets.

Helmbander German, the metal plates or scrolls carrying mottos

Hatchet. Arm badge worn by pioneers of Foot Guards

Helmet. Dragoon Guards and Dragoons from 1871 to 1914

or honours placed on a helmet.

Helmet A protective covering for the head, usually of metal but occasionally of leather.

Hessians An elegant type of light boot which finished below the knee with a 'v' notch in front, popular at the beginning of the 19th century but continued to be worn by light cavalrymen in the 20th century.

HG These initials worn within a laurel wreath on the lower arm indicate a soldier qualified as a Hotchkiss gunner. See also 'machine gunners'.

Highland dress After the Restoration the first British troops to wear Highland dress were the companies of the Black Watch who were regimented in 1739. Other Highland regiments were raised – Loudon, Montgomery, Fraser, Keith and Campbell, etc. – in all eleven regiments which were disbanded by 1763. In 1775 the formation of many new Highland regiments was begun but most were disbanded at the end of the American Revolutionary War. In 1787 the 74th and the 75th Foot were raised and in 1793/4 eight new regiments of Highlanders came into being. Despite the law forbidding Highland dress these Highland regiments wore the full dress, kilt, bonnet, etc.

In modern times Lowland regiments have adopted items of dress once considered as Highland and many pipe bands continue to wear the complete dress including the feather bonnet even though full dress is not authorised. Also for parts of the Highland dress, see under separate headings, e.g. bonnet, feather bonnet, glengarry, doublet, kilt, plaid, hose etc. etc.

Hoheitsabzeichen German, devices and signs of distinction for higher formation worn by German forces in the time of Nazi rule; the Nazi eagle and swastika in various shapes.

Holes This expression to be seen in tailors' books of the 18th and 19th century referred to button-holes (q.v.).

Holster Once part of horse equipment but later accepted for the pistol or revolver holster carried on the person.

Holster-caps On the horse the open end of the holster was sometimes covered with fur, skin or a flap of cloth. In some regulations these are referred to as caps, which might be confused with caps worn by cavalrymen or grenadiers.

Home service helmet When the shako was being worn at home by British troops a tropical helmet was being worn at some foreign stations. With the acceptance of a white helmet it was decided in 1877 that a blue cloth helmet similar in shape to the overseas helmet should be produced for 'home service'. No doubt the change from shako to helmet was prompted by the defeat of the French kepi by the German pickelhaube in the Franco-Prussian War.

Horizon blue The colour chosen by the French Army for its service dress. This shade of blue-grey had been tested before 1912 but the French troops entered the First World War in blue and

Horseshoe. Arm badge of farrier

red. Before the end of 1914 the new uniform was being produced in quantity and worn extensively in Spring 1915. It continued in favour until 1935.

Horn button This type of button was favoured by riflemen because it merged with their dark uniform much better than the bright pewter or brass of other infantry. Horn buttons were later replaced with composition buttons as worn by rifle regiments today.

Horse shoe The badge of a horse shoe was worn in the 18th century as the trade badge of a farrier. At first on the headdress, it moved to the arm by 1864 where it may be seen today on the right upper arm even in the case of qualified senior NCOs.

Hose May refer to the German for trousers (usually *hosen*). In the British Army the word chiefly refers to the hose worn by the Scottish troops from the 18th century onwards. Originally in red and white, a black line was added later to heighten the crossing stripes. In early Victorian times red and green hose (Rob Roy) appeared. Cloth hose (cath datch, q.v.) was worn until about 1848 when stocking or knitted hose was introduced.

Hose tops When the 'moggan' (q.v.) became a hose top is not clear but the footless hose (or half-hose) was needed as the stiff 'cath dath' was not suitable for long marches. The arrival of khaki also affected the colour of the Highlanders' hose and khaki hose tops were worn also by other infantry in the East. Different colours were further permitted and an ACI of 1956 noted scarlet with blue legs, all yellow, primrose, various shades of green, crimson and other colours apart from tartan.

Horse Regiments of horse in the British Army were the heavy cavalry of the line which later converted to dragoon guards or in the case of the Royal Regiment of Horse became the Royal Horse Guards (Blue). Originally they rode heavy horses for weighty cavalry charges and were armed with swords and protected by iron breastplates. They wore dark red coats with differing facings in the long lapels and the cuffs.

Housings The cloth furniture on horses which could include the saddlecloth (or shabraque) as well as the holster caps.

Hue Danish for cap.

Hummel, humble Scottish. The round woollen cap worn by Highlanders, normally blue with a red tuft (or tourie) on top. Originally in the modern bonnet style, it could be altered even to cover a shako as in the case of the Highland Light Infantry.

Hunting Stuart (Stewart) This tartan has been worn by the Royal Scots since 1901 in place of the Grant tartan (see also Royal Stuart tartan).

Hussar The light horseman of Hungary were named 'huszar' which was said to have come from the Italian 'corsare' a corsair or freebooter and date back to the 14th century when *ussari* were in Polish pay. Two hussar regiments were in the Bavarian army of the Blue Kings and France had her light cavalry by 1692. Great

Britain acquired her hussars by converting light dragoon regiments and by 1805 the new dress was recognisable. It was the fur cap or the mirliton (q.v.) which made the final change. The fur-lined pelisse derived from the wolf-skin cloak of the Hungarian came to Britain in the late 18th century. The sabretache (the pocket attached to the sabre-belt) was necessary in the case of hussars because the very tight trousers did not permit pockets. The light cavalry boot (Hessian) was much more satisfactory than the heavy jacked boot of heavy cavalry. The last full dress of hussars maintained most of the original features although the pelisse disappeared at the time of the Crimean War and the sabretache went at the death of Queen Victoria.

Hut German for hat.

I

Imperial Crown. As introduced in reign of King Edward VII

IC These letters appear on certain drivers' arm badges after the First World War to indicate knowledge of the Internal Combustion engine but these badges had a short life.

Imperial Crown The crown introduced by King Edward VII in 1901 has sometimes been called the Imperial Crown. Official documents called it the Tudor 'Henry VII' crown. There was however an Imperial Crown chosen by Queen Victoria. This seems to have been inspired by Her Majesty becoming Empress of India. The arches of the 'Hanoverian' crown were simplified, each being reduced to an almost straight line instead of the earlier more subtle curves.

Imperial Cypher On becoming Empress of India, Queen Victoria added an 'I' to her 'VR' cypher and this 'VRI' often appears on Indian badges and insignia. 'ERI' and 'GRI' are cyphers appropriate for later monarchs.

Indian pattern serge Light-weight serge frocks (q.v.) were worn in India in the latter part of the 19th century.

Initials This term normally refers to the letters embroidered or in metal on the shoulder-straps of the soldier's tunic or coat. However the Foot Guards refer to their initials as numerals.

Instructor There is no specific badge for an instructor in the British Army but various instructors have their own distinguishing badge, like the grenade for Royal Engineers which also has 'QI' and other branches like artillery, weapon training, signalling, parachuting, etc. which are described elsewhere.

Instrument case A case to hold surgeon's instruments was carried on the shoulder-belt of medical officers in late Victorian times. In modern times canvas cases were made for instruments used by artillerymen and engineers.

Intrim attila German, an undress tunic.

Inverness flap When the Scottish doublet was introduced after the Crimean War, it was not given the normal skirts, but four flaps to correspond with the ancient 'four-tailed' doublet or coat. The front flaps had three buttons and loops on each.

Invisible green This term was applied to riflemen's clothing in the late 19th century but the actual colour often appeared as black.

Isabella This was a colour popular in the French Army in the 18th century for facings and regimental colours. This light buff colour is said to originate according to an unflattering story from the colour of Queen Isabella's dirty undergarments.

Ivory Stick An ebony stick tipped with ivory issued to 'brigadiers' of Charles II's Guards, being junior to the gold and silver stick (q.v.). The Harbinger of the Gentlemen-at-Arms also had an ivory stick.

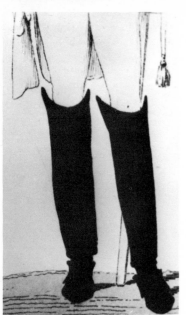

Jack boots. As worn by heavy cavalry, c.1812

Jacket. Officer of 6th Dragoon Guards, c.1804

Jack boots Stout cavalry boots which have been 'jacked', a process which involved wax and tar to make a hard surface.

Jacket From a 'jack' (a coat). These short coats were adopted by light infantry and light cavalry about the middle of the 18th century in order to give them more freedom of movement. The 1784 light cavalry jacket was more like a sleeved waistcoat over which was a sleeveless shell. The subsequent patterns for light cavalry were also short without skirts, although about 1812 the patterns have very short tails behind. Linen jackets were worn for undress occasions and the white fatigue (q.v.) jacket continued until the Second World War.

Jampot cuff This was the name given to the simple round cuff of other ranks' tunic from about 1882 to 1902.

Jangees (janghers) Short drawers worn by the Indian foot soldier in the 18th and 19th centuries.

Jeff Davis hat General Jefferson C. Davis when Secretary for War was responsible for the issue of black felt hats for the army in 1858. Although Major Hardee may have initiated the prototype, the nickname was the 'Jeff Davis' hat.

Jersey Khaki jerseys and pullovers were worn in the First World War but were purchased privately and not subject to regulation. In the Second World War not only were jersey and pullovers worn officially for cold climates but also in the Middle East over khaki drill shirts. In Korea heavy woollen jerseys were needed for the cold weather. The 'No. 13 Dress' introduced in November 1971 included the heavy jersey for officers with plain worsted

Jacket. Officer of Royal Horse Artillery, *c.*1815

Jungle hat. Worn in many shapes in Far East

badges of rank on the shoulders. Unofficially or otherwise many colours of jerseys have appeared in modern times: black for the Royal Armoured Corps, dark blue for the Royal Artillery and Royal Signals, various shades of green and even a dark maroon for the 4/7 Dragoon Guards.

Jodhpur Indian cavalry breeches, tight in the leg but loose elsewhere.

Jungle hat A 'deerstalker' hat made of fabric had been experimentally worn before the Second World War. When a hat was needed in 1942 for the Far East, this type was used for training purposes. The green jungle-clothing introduced in June 1944 included a deerstalker hat. This continued in use, specially as it was much cheaper than the old sun helmet which had been declared obsolete. Even this soft headdress which could stand up to rough treatment received embellishments in the form of twisted turbans or regimental colour patches on the side.

Jungle boot The radical re-organisation of uniform and equipment needed for jungle warfare brought the jungle boot into being. This had a cloth or canvas upper with a lace-up front, so made that the wearer could wade through water and yet avoid such hazards as leeches and other tropical troubles.

Jungle green The light khaki drill first used in the Far East was found unsuitable in the darkness of the green jungles. Thus the new jungle cloth was not only tough but of a dark green shade that was colour-fast and good for camouflage purposes. Web equipment was also made in the same colour.

Jupanek German, a kind of sleeved waistcoat with standing collar worn by the Leib-Ulan-Eskadron.

Justacorp French, a long body coat worn in the 17th century by infantry men.

Kaftan, caftan From the Turkish quftan. A long Eastern garment with sleeves which came over the hand. A style adopted by many European armies at the end of the 17th century.

Kalpak, calpac A fur cap with a cloth crown worn in Russia and Turkey.

Kamarband, kummerbund etc. See 'cummerbund'.

Kamisol German, see 'camisole'.

Kapotte German (also *kapuze*) cloth hood or covering for the head which could be brought forward from the back of the collar of the overcoat.

Kaputrocke, caputrock German, a loose-fitting, double-breasted coat worn in the Austrian army in the 18th and 19th centuries. Evolved from the **kaputfrocke**, a kneelength frockcoat.

Kartuche German, for cartridge.

Kartache-kasten German, for cartridge box.

Kashmir hose Long white cashmir breeches worn by Prussian generals in the 19th century.

Kepi French, from *kappe*, originally a soft cap with a peak in front. Later stiffened and given rows of braid to indicate the rank of the wearer.

Key When seen in British badges it is an indication that the regiment had been in the great Siege of Gibraltar (q.v.) when a sally into the enemy's lines resulted in the capture of the arsenal and the keys. In America the badge of a key crossed with a sword indicates the Quartermaster Corps.

Kerseymere The name used in the 18th and 19th centuries for cassimere – usually a white soft cloth for breeches and linings.

Kessel pawker German, kettledrum.

Kettledrummer In the British Army the kettledrummer had no special badge but he did wear the dress of the cavalry bandsmen. In the case of the 3rd Dragoons (later the 3rd Hussars) the kettledrummer had a special distinction because at the end of the 18th century he was a negro and wore a silver collar around his neck; a tradition of a silver collar is still maintained in the regiment.

Khaki Based on the Persian or Indian word for 'dust' the use of khaki as a service dress is a British innovation which has spread all round the world. It was the Corps of Guides raised in India in 1846 who are said to have first dyed their clothes with river mud. The actual colour varies but when the British Army adopted khaki serge for a fighting dress in 1896 it was more akin to the colour worn today.

Khoger Native saddlery used in India.

Kilmarnock The town in Scotland where bonnets have been made for the British Army at least since 1800. A type of Kilmar-

Kettledrummer. 4th Queen's Own Hussars, 1911

Kilmarnock. As worn by Royal Scots, *c.*1904

nock was worn by the English soldier from about 1812 up to 1874. The diced bonnet as now worn by Scottish soldiers is made in Kilmarnock. A specific type of Kilmarnock is that adopted by the Royal Scots and the King's Own Scottish Borderers in 1903 as a full dress item. This was stiffened and cocked high on the left side with a large rosette and a plume of black-cock feathers. The regimental badge was on the rosette. These special types became obsolete in 1939 when officers' full dress was discontinued.

Kilt The pleated garment worn on a waistband by Scottish soldiers. (Also worn by Greek evzones who are also highlanders.) It is pleated at back and sides with a flat front piece overlapping and fastening on the right, either with a brooch, a blanket pin or rosettes. See also the breccan, feilebeg and plaid.

Kitt Upper jacket, see 'pelisse'.

Kittel German, a loose upper garment worn by soldiers in arsenals and for drill purposes, in the 18th and 19th centuries. Russian soldiers wore the kittel up to 1910 after which officers wore a smarter version.

Kittle A garment or coat worn by sergeant-drummers in William III's reign.

Kiwa, kiwer A distinctive type of shako with a dip or angle on the top introduced in the early 19th century for the Russian Army. After a long lapse, the kiwer was re-introduced in 1910 to the Russian army but the outbreak of the First World War gave it a short life.

Kleeblatt German, a braid ornament which finished in three loops suggesting a clover leaf.

Kleiner dienstanzug German, undress uniform.

Knapsack From the German, a sack to carry necessaries. In the 18th century a goatskin bag with straps was carried over the shoulders. The container developed into a more rigid shape with buckled straps.

Kneeboots Boots coming to just below the knee. A pattern introduced in April 1896 for mounted men had five pairs of eyelets to be laced at the instep. Other patterns of kneeboots were worn previously.

Knee pads The pads to strap on the leg do not seem to have ever been an official issue. The purpose was to protect the knee when kneeling to fire a musket or rifle. They were known to be in use by the 61st Foot in India as early as 1856.

Knickerbockers A type of breeches. In 1883 the Madras Army took into wear a new uniform which included knickerbockers either of serge or khaki. The 1885 Dress Regulations quote the full dress version as being black with scarlet sidestripes. The khaki version were made loose at the waist and legs similar to pyjamas and the waist adjusted to the body by means of a piece of tape running through the waistband. The bottom of the legs reached to the ankles and puttees or gaiters were expected to be worn.

Knopfarben German, colour of the buttons – gold or silver (or

Knot. Stafford knot in badge of 64th Foot

Knot as worn with sword

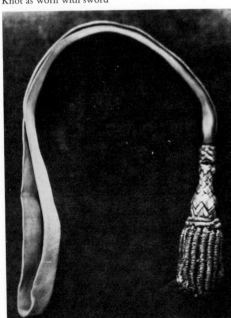

yellow or white) so that they matched the braid or lace.

Knot The knot took many forms in army dress. (a) The shoulder knot (which in the 17th century could be of ribbon) kept the sword-belt from slipping off the shoulder. It was still in use in the middle of the 18th century by when it had taken a formalised shape and was placed just behind the right shoulder. The arrival of the shoulder-strap and the epaulette caused the shoulder-knot to go out of fashion; (b) the sword knot though now an ornament had been a practical item when first worn. The strap which was firmly attached to the sword hilt and guard was long enough for the loop to go over the hand and wrist, so that if a sword was knocked out of the hand, it did not fall to the ground, but hung safely from the arm. Leather sword-knots were used by cavalrymen. The later gold or silver braid knot was just about functional. The regular army had gold wire with a crimson thread (to indicate the Cross of St George) and others had silver wire with crimson. In Germany silver wire and black thread indicated the Prussian colours; (c) the knot on the sash or scarf was needed to keep the sash in position and it is said that the shoulder sash also supported the sword from the knot. Later when the sash was tied around the waist, an order of 1768 placed the knot on the right side for cavalry and on the left for infantry; (d) the ornamental shaping of cord, braid or gimp on a tunic was sometimes given a special name like the Austrian Knot which had three complicated loops on the cuff; (e) the knot appears in badges, most notably in Staffordshire units where the Stafford Knot (an open knot with two loose ends) has local application.

Kokarde German, cockade. When on the black leather helmet the Reich cockade (black, white and red) was on the right side and the *landeskokarde* on the left. Cockades in national colours were normally worn on the upper part of the undress cap.

Koller German, a full dress cavalry coat fastened down the front with hooks and eyes, usually with a trimming around the collar, cuffs and down the front.

Kollett German, a double-breasted coatee worn from 1806 by all cavalrymen. In full dress the cut was changed by an Army order of 1843. The early laced pattern was very similar to the British Light Dragoon pattern introduced in 1812.

Kolpak German, fur cap or busby.

Konfederatka cap This was the name given to the ancient peasant cap worn by the men of Cracow. The four-sided flat top was the origin of the lancer cap made so popular by the Polish lancers of the Napoleonic era.

Kopfbedeckung German, head-covering, headdress.

Koppel German, sword strap or knot.

Kordon German, cords as on shako or headdress.

Kossuth Louis Kossuth, the Hungarian patriot who visited the U.S.A., wore a broad-brimmed black hat and so the nickname of the Kossuth hat became yet another name for the headdress of the

Kukris. Crossed kukris badge worn by 14/20th Hussars

Civil War period. See Jeff Davis and Hardee.

Kragen German, collar.

Kragenpatte German, collar patch.

Kukris Although it may be expected that kukris may feature in badges of the Gurkhas, they also appear in British units. The 14/20th Hussars had a wartime association with the Gurkhas in the Second World War and thus wear a small metal badge of crossed kukris on the arm.

Kulla, kullah Small close-fitting Indian cap, generally pointed and usually worn as the base for a turban.

Kürass German, for cuirass.

Kurta, kurtah Loose frock or blouse worn in India, reaching to the knees, with neck opening to the waist.

Kwaster Netherlands, tassel on cord worn as a sign of rank. Also on trumpet cords.

Kuzzlebash A Persian headdress, also worn by some Indian cavalry.

L

Lamb. The Paschal Lamb on badge of Queen's Royal Surrey Regiment

Lance cap. Officer, 12th Lancers, c.1855

L The initial 'L' within laurel is the arm badge for 'layers' in the artillery, introduced in 1892 and still worn.

Lace Although this word may apply to many aspects of clothing, it is mainly used to indicate the gold and silver braids ornamenting officers' clothing. The flat braid could be woven in a variety of patterns such as rose, thistle, shamrock and a great number of geometrical designs as 'broken bias', 'ess and vellum', French check and scallop. Regimental lace could be worn on the coatee, tunic, waistcoat and trousers as well as the headdress in the 19th century. The gold lace chevrons worn by NCOs are one of the remaining examples of the ancient craft, although the State Dress of the Household Cavalry bands has many ancient patterns. See also 'braid', 'black line'.

Lagermütze German, camp cap, a cloth cap worn in undress.

Lamb The badge of a Lamb was the special badge of the 2nd Foot, originally the Queen's (Catherine of Braganza) Regiment of Foot. The nickname of Kirke's Lambs goes back to their first colonel. There was another regiment at an earlier period also known as the 'Lambs', the men of Lord Musgrave who wore white coats. It is said that the lamb was a special animal connected with Queen Catherine of Braganza but that has been difficult to prove.

Lambskin These were used as horse furniture, even after the cloth shabraque was abolished. Cavalry patrol jackets were lined with astrakhan which was lambskin. A lambskin busby was worn by officers of the 60th Rifles from 1873 to 1881 when the helmet superseded it.

Lance (a) The weapon frequently appears in metal badges of lancer regiments but it is not always part of a badge for their arm; (b) for those proficient in lance exercise, there were prize badges, going from crossed lances for the 3rd class, to lances and star for 2nd class and lances, crown and wreath for the 1st class. They were discontinued when horses became obsolete on the outbreak of the Second World War.

Lance cap, lancer cap Although popular on the Continent, lancers were not introduced into the British Army until 1816. The lance cap was based on the Polish four-sided cap (see 'Konfederatka cap') and was distinguished by the colour of the top (usually the facing colour), the plate and the plume.

Lancers In the British Army regiments of lancers wore blue coatees with plastrons (q.v.) the colour of the facings. William IV wished the British Army to appear as much as possible in red coats and lancers changed to this colour in 1831. In 1840 when Queen Victoria was on the throne, the original blue colour was restored

Laurel. Wreath of laurel leaves on shako-plate, 84th Foot, c.1870

except in the case of the 16th Lancers who retained the red coat and were known as the 'Scarlet Lancers'. This distinction remained to the end of full dress.

Langetuchehosen German, undress trousers.

Lanyard A lanyard could be worn by a cavalryman in the 19th century for his revolver or by an artilleryman to fire his gun. The use of the lanyard is now mainly ornamental but serves to distinguish a regiment or a corps. The cord around the arm and under the shoulder-strap may be single, double or plaited. Officers often have thick lanyards or cords of twisted silk with a brass snap fastener.

Lanzen-flagge German, for pennant or lance-flag.

Lapel When the long loose coat had the fronts turned back in the 18th century they formed lapels of the facing colour. Regiments of horse had the lapels all the way down to the bottom of the coat, light cavalry and infantry had half lapels. By the end of the century it again became the fashion to button the coat over the chest in a double-breasted style. The lapels could be worn with the facing colours showing or even with only a small part with two triangles turned down at the top just below the collar. The introduction of the tunic saw the abandonment of lapels although the lancer plastron, a form of lapels, continued in use.

Laurel The use of laurel leaves or wreath is extensive in army badges following the Roman practice of wearing laurels or bay leaves as a mark of military honour. Thus laurels appear on rank badges of general officers, on many regimental badges, belt-plates and buttons, as well as on tradesmen's badges. On the tradesmen's many arm badges what is called a laurel wreath is actually two sprays of laurel leaves for they do not meet at the top but have a wide gap.

Layer The qualification for an artilleryman (or other soldier) who 'lays' a gun or heavy weapon is the initial 'L' within laurel as an arm badge.

Leading staff The leading staff was a stick with an ornamental head, often of silver with tassels used by officers leading his men. This may have been a small version of the partisan and was used by the Honourable Artillery Company as late as the first quarter of the 18th century. It appears as part of the crest in the coat-of-arms of that Company and has been worn as a badge.

Leaf See Oakleaf.

Leather cap This term was applied to the full dress or undress caps or shakos worn in the first part of the 19th century by European and American troops.

Leather stock A cravat or a piece of cloth had been worn around the soldier's neck to act both as collar and tie. In the 18th century when an upright soldier was desired, a leather stock around the neck helped to keep the soldier's head high. This stock was a band of stiff leather with buckles and fastening at the back of the neck.

Leggings These leg coverings can range from short black gaiters

Leopardskin. Bass-drummer, Fusiliers, *c.*1897

to the long leggings worn by cavalrymen. Usually made of leather the short versions were to be worn by all dismounted British soldiers in 1862. The cavalry versions were numerous including the sto'wasser and were popular in the South African War and later.

Leibrock German, dress coat or cavalry coat.

Leopard skin The troops serving overseas, especially those in India, had opportunities of acquiring leopard skins and these were adapted to military purposes. In 1785 officers of the Light Dragoons were permitted to line their upper jackets with fur (thus producing an early form of pelisse) and the 16th Light Dragoons chose to use leopard skins although these were discontinued a few years later. It is possible that light dragoon sabretaches at the end of the 18th century were covered with leopard skin. In the 19th century it was customary for officers of Hussars to have leopard skins as part of their horse furniture, the 1894 Dress Regulations naming 12 regiments so distinguished. Infantry regiments had little opportunity for such extravagance but occasionally bass drummers and tenor drummers might sport these skins as protective aprons, in the case of the bass drummer including the animal's head.

Levée dress This elaborate dress wore at levées and evening functions frequently allowed for the use of the cocked hat and for colourful netherwear not worn on any other occasion. When full dress was restored for officers after the First World War, they were permitted to wear this for the attending of levées, until the Second World War brought about the discontinuance of their full dress.

Lewis gunner The popular employment of the Lewis (machine) gun in the First World War brought into use an arm badge with 'LG' and laurels. The badge for the 1st Class Lewis gunner was authorised under an Army Order of 1917 and in 1921 was widened to include all light machine gunners.

LG These initials and laurels were first the arm badge of Lewis gunners and then in 1921 for all light machine gunners. For Territorial men before the Second World War 'LG' without laurel was worn but with the addition of stars or a crown to indicate degrees of proficiency. Today 'LMG' for light machine gun is worn.

Light This is the space between stripes or pieces of lace. It may be the foundation cloth or material actually joining the two stripes and sometimes a contrasting colour like that of the facings.

Light companies The use of solid masses of infantry in battle was not practical in colonial warfare and the use of detached and quick-moving troops was popular by 1759. To permit rapid movement the coats were cut down to jackets, the brim of the cocked hat was reduced and the gaiters made to reach only to the calf. The armament was lighter and even the drum was changed to a hunting horn for the purpose of signals. Constant experiment with headdresses produced some interesting leather caps with feathers or tufts of hair. Wings were put on the shoulders of the coat and these remained until about 1857 when flank companies were abolished.

Light Dragoon. Officer, 8th Hussars, 1820

In the 19th century the men's shakos were similar to the battalion companies but had their own colour for tuft or ball.

Light dragoons These light cavalrymen were introduced into the British Army about the same time as the light companies, and also had 'lightened' clothing. Smaller men were chosen and lighter cavalry boots were worn. The caps were either metal or leather but by the time of the American Revolution a new helmet, later called the Tarleton, was adopted which had a bearskin crest going over the top but was replaced by a broad-topped shako in 1812. Light dragoons now wore jackets with a plastron front. They followed in the infantry styles of headdress but by 1861 all light dragoons had been converted to hussars.

Light Infantry The creation of light troops in Great Britain began in 1758. By 1759 not only were there light companies raised but complete regiments such as Gage's 80th Foot and Morgan's 90th. These regiments were disbanded but others were created sometimes from existing regiments. The 90th Perthshire Volunteers raised in 1794 as light infantry all wore leather caps or helmets but other later regiments had the shako with distinctions of green. During 1879–81 when the Germanic helmet was adopted light infantry wore a green helmet. They also wore wings on their coats until the Crimean War. Whistles were carried on the shoulder-belts of officers and NCOs in order to give field commands when the bugle was not used.

Line Regiments of Cavalry With the exception of the Household Cavalry all cavalry was of the Line. They were eventually divided into Dragoon Guards (which had been Regiments of Horse) numbered one to seven and the remainder Dragoons, Hussars and Lancers (the last two once being light dragoons) numbered up to 21 at the end of Queen Victoria's reign. Although dragoons originally were mounted infantry, they became grouped with the heavy cavalry. There were distinctive dresses for dragoon guards, dragoons, light dragoons, hussars and lancers; for uniform of each, see under own heading.

Line Regiments of Infantry This category does not include the Foot Guards which are Royal regiments of the sovereign. There are also Royal Regiments in the Line like the Royal Scots who wear facing of the Royal blue. Up to 1747 British regiments were known by their colonel's name. Although they had been given a precedence, the sequence of numbers was not made permanent until 1747. The numbers in late Victorian times reached 109 plus the Rifle Brigade. Highland and Lowland regiments, light infantry, fusiliers and rifle regiments were all included somewhat haphazardly with the rest of the line, taking their precedence from date of raising or when they entered service with England. In 1881 'territorial' names were used instead of the old numbers so badges and titles on uniforms changed. Over the years the headdress ranged from the hat, through the various shakoes up to the helmet of 1879, with other headdress for special regiments.

Light Infantry. Cap of light infantry company, 5th Foot, c.1779

Line Cavalry. Officer, 2nd Dragoon Guards, *c.*1900

Linen collar These white collars were worn with undress uniform of the 7th Hussars and the Oxfordshire Light Infantry (as noted in the 1900 Dress Regulations). When the style of mess dress changed to the open neck jacket then the white skirt and collar were worn. White strip collars were worn with the long frock coat. When the Coronation Blues were introduced in 1937 a strip of white collar was worn above the blue tunic collar.

Litewka (from Polish) Originally a long-skirted outdoor coat but later it became a shorter garment like a tunic although the 1903 grey pattern was not waisted.

Litzen German, braid as on patches of collar and cuffs.

Livery coats Although the wearing of livery is expected for servants of nobility, many early commanders of soldiers were noblemen and gave their livery to drummers, trumpeters and other military musicians. Normally the heraldic colours and metals of a coat-of-arms were chosen and the elaborate coat was often covered with much braid and ornamentation. This influence was to be noted for military music in the 18th and 19th centuries. In modern times simplifications and economy bring the ordinary soldier's coat to the musician with the possible addition of wings.

LMG A variation of the many 'gunnery' badges is that of the 'LMG' and laurels of the light machine gunner worn in the reigns of King George VI and Queen Elizabeth II. It was on the left forearm usually of khaki but also with grounds of regimental colours like the red of the King's Royal Rifle Corps.

Locket This type of waistbelt fastening was common for officers in the 19th century and the central disc usually carried regimental devices. The circular piece of one side (the male section) fitted into the open circlet of the other side (the female section) to make a firm fastening. The advent of the crimson sash around the officer's waist in 1902 made the locket obsolete. In May 1850 the private soldier was to discontinue the bayonet belt worn over the right shoulder and to wear a waistbelt with a locket. The other ranks' locket plate had the Royal Crest in the centre with the motto 'DIEU ET MON DROIT' on the circlet. Scottish regiments had the sejant Scottish Lion in the centre and 'IN DEFENSE' on the circlet.

Long service stripe These are really long service and good conduct awards. They take the form of chevrons although called stripes and are worn on the lower arm with the points upwards.

Loop A military term which varies in detail over the centuries. The 'loop-ed clothing' of grenadiers in the 17th century referred to the braid loops surrounding the button-holes of the coat. The braid or tape later on the soldiers' coat was of distinctive patterns and weaves intended to identify a particular regiment. The spacing of the loops (regular, in pairs or threes) also permitted further distinction. Loops in the 19th century were frequently non-essential as some buttons had no button-holes. The gorget which hung from ribbons tied at the back of the neck, later had ribbons which 'looped' over the buttons on the side of the collar.

Lyre. Embroidered arm badge of Royal Artillery bandsmen.

Lowland dress For many years the Highland dress was demonstrated by that worn with the kilt. Gradually in the time of Queen Victoria tartan trews marked some Scottish regiments and eventually the Lowland regiments had trews, doublets and for headdress a shako or the new-styled Kilmarnock of Edward VII's reign.

Lungi, loongi, longhi Indian, originally a waist cloth but now synonymous with *pugri*. The *lungi* was often tied loosely and appeared much longer than the turban.

Lyre The badge of a lyre was chosen to distinguish British bandmasters and bandsmen. The Royal Artillery have had their own pattern of lyre from 1856 up to the present day. Infantry bandsmen had their new pattern lyre from 1907 onwards. Bandmasters' lyres usually had extra foliage. The Royal Military School of Music had their own pattern for the student bandsmen.

Machinegun. Metal badge of Machine Gun Corps

M The arm badge of an 'M' and laurel is a post-war introduction for the qualification of 'mortarman'. It is worn on the left forearm on a variety of background colours. Apart from the normal khaki, there is black on green, black on scarlet and green on maize. There was also an arm badge of a red 'M' around a bullet which was the sign of a marksman in the Volunteer Training Corps of the First World War.

Mace Although the drum-majors of infantry carry a mace or staff, it is not worn as a badge.

Machine gun The crossed barrels of a machine gun were the badge of the corps when created in 1915. The heavy section which wore this badge became the Tank Corps in 1917. The Machine Gun Corps was disbanded in 1922.

Machine gunners Although there may have been no special uniform of machine gunners as they only served when khaki was worn, there were certain arm badges which they could have to denote proficiency and in fact those worn later when the Machine Gun Corps was disbanded, such as 'LG' (Lewis gunners), 'HG' (Hotchkiss gunners), 'LMG', 'SMG', all of which see under own heading.

Maltese Cross The true Maltese Cross has eight points of which the four arms meet in the centre as sharp points. The cross patée or formée was used by rifle corps from the end of the 18th century as a badge but it has been most probably called a Maltese Cross because Ferdinand Hompesch who in 1796 raised riflemen who became the 5th Battalion, King's Royal Rifle Corps, may have been a relation of Ferdinand de Hompesch, the last Grand Master of the Knights of Malta. British rifle corps adopted the eight-pointed cross as one of their regimental badges.

Mameluke Originally Turkish and Circassian slaves, these men became established as a fighting body in Egypt. After Napoleon invaded that country, he employed some Mamelukes as his own guard and in 1804 they added much colour to parades when they still wore their oriental dress. The campaign in Egypt encouraged adoption by the British of some local distinctions, one in particular being the Mameluke sword favoured by cavalrymen, occasionally infantry officers and remaining in wear until the 20th century by general officers with the simple gilt cross guards and white hilt.

Manteau French, cloak or mantel.

Maple leaf The official badge of Canada, a small metal version was worn on the upper arm by British troops of the 25th Tank Brigade after they served with the 1st Canadian Corps in the Second World War.

Marketenden German, sutler, also *marketenderin*, canteen-wo-

Marksman. Embroidered badge of First World War

Mercury. Embroidered badge as worn over sergeant's chevrons in Royal Corps of Signals

man, q.v. 'cantinière'.

Marksman There were various distinctions to mark a soldier proficient with a firearm. In mid-Victorian times an arm badge worn on the right sleeve of crossed muskets was awarded for three grades of prizes for skill-at-arms. These were later changed to the proficiency category. In the Second World War a sniper's arm badge was the muskets or rifles plus the letter 's'. Volunteer Training Corps of the same period had their own arm badge, that of an 'M' intertwined around a bullet. Just before World War I the badges for good shooting were increased to five – crossed muskets for marksman, muskets and stars for best shot in squadron company or band, muskets and crown for section commanders, muskets, star and wreath for best shot corporal etc. in regiment or battalion, muskets, crown and wreath for best shot sergeant or lance-sergeant in regiment or battalion. Only the crown and muskets were worn on the right arms, the others were worn on the left. After that war the term musket was replaced by rifle. Volunteer and territorial soldiers and cadets had their own distinctions for good shooting.

Marshal Although used as a high rank on the continent, Great Britain always had the rank of Field Marshal (q.v.).

Match This is the twisted material which was kept burning when a 'matchlock' musketeer was in action. It could be stowed in the hat, wound round the belt or wound round the hand in action.

Matchcase It became the custom in the 17th and 18th centuries for soldiers, particularly grenadiers, to have a perforated tin or brass tube on the shoulder-belt, inside which the burning end of the match could be kept alight. By the middle of the 18th century it was obsolete and was officially abolished in 1784.

Maud The maud was a grey striped plaid worn by Highland and Border shepherds and in 1771 it was stated that the maud (maude) would be a proper covering for light infantry in place of a blanket. Pictures of the 25th Foot (a Lowland regiment) in the Mediterranean area about this period show the maud being worn as a cloak.

MC These letters embroidered in khaki within laurels and combined with a winged wheel indicate a motorcycle driver, c.1914.

Medals Although decorations may have been worn earlier by officers it was not until the 18th century that medals were granted to other ranks (actually in India in base metal for the natives). Waterloo was the first battle for which all British troops were issued with a medal, those for the Peninsular Wars being issued much later in Queen Victoria's time when many possible recipients were dead. Medals were to be worn on uniforms on special occasions but the wearing of pieces of medal ribbon was allowed at all times. These varied in depth even up to an inch wide but at the end of the 19th century they were reduced to a narrow depth.

Meldtaschen German, for despatch case or pouch.

Mercury The figure of Mercury (nicknamed 'Jimmy') is the Greek god chosen as the messenger of the Gods and worn as a badge by the Royal Corps of Signals. It is also worn above the sergeant's stripes.

Mermaid The Mermaid of Warsaw appears on the embroidered arm badge worn by men of the 7th Queen's Own Hussars on the left sleeve. It is an honour gained in 1945 when the regiment served with the 2nd Polish Corps in Italy.

Mess dress The introduction and development of mess dress was slow and gradual, brought about by the wish to have a comfortable dress worn in the mess and at dinners. At the beginning of the 19th century at least one cavalry regiment wore an open jacket with the sash and belt underneath. In 1828 the shell or undress jacket was worn in the Indian messes and the fashion gradually spread to the United Kingdom. The open mess jacket allowed a fancy regimental waistcoat to be worn and many regiments had their own pattern. At first the waistcoat was closed to the neck, often with a stand collar but later a white shirt and black tie was worn with a low-cut waistcoat. The mess jacket also took other forms, sometimes with a roll collar and big revers. The dress then became subject to regulation not only for officers but also for sergeants and others.

Mess tin Actually part of equipment rather than uniform, sometimes with white or black coverings.

Messingschuppenketten German, brass scale chin strap.

MG Within laurel sprays for the arm badge of a machine gunner. In the First World War the embroidered badge denoted a 1st Class machine gunner. By the Second World War it indicated a medium machine gunner.

Militia Although the militia was created long before the Standing Army the uniforms of the latter led the fashion. The militia were locally clothed but expected to follow the regular army styles. In 1830 it was decided that gold lace should be worn only by the regular army and that silver lace was to be worn by officers of the militia. When the Territorial scheme of 1881 linked the militia battalions as 3rd or 4th battalions of the regulars, officers were all allowed to have gold with the distinction of a small 'M' on the shoulder cords and/or badge to denote militia. The militia brought many special badges to the regular infantry regiments where before there had been no more than a number. In a further re-organisation in 1908 the role of the militia declined into a reserve capacity. They did not fight as a regiment in the First World War but operated on a reserve and supply basis, fading away after the war finished.

Mirliton A tall felt cap worn by French light cavalry inspired by the oriental headdress – the *haiduk* and worn up to the time of Napoleon (see also *flügel mutze*).

Mittens Normally a loose hand-covering with a thumb but no fingers for use in cold weather. In military use one finger is often made separate for firing a rifle or for reins.

MM These initials combined with laurel as an arm badge after the First World War to indicate a Motor Mechanic.

Mirliton. Worn by French hussar, *c.*1800

Moccasins Although originally Red Indian foot coverings, these soft leather shoes are used in Canadian winters, in fact snowshoes can only be used with the moccasin.

Moggins These Scottish items are footless hose, worn in marching order at the beginning of the 19th century. Also worn with socks and garters.

Mohair A stiff braid from the wool of the Angora goat, utilised as a decoration on coats usually for undress.

Montur German, meaning uniform.

Morocco Leather dressed in this fashion became popular in the Napoleonic campaigns in Egypt. Morocco leather is used for belts and backings to sabretaches.

Mortar men The use of simple mortars (little more than hollow tubes) in the First World War brought into use trained men who wore a badge of a blue grenade on the upper arm. Since the Second World War the use of mortars has again developed and the mortar men wear an embroidered 'M' and laurels on various coloured backgrounds on the left forearm.

Motor cyclist Wore an embroidered arm badge with 'MC' (q.v.). The soft cap of the First World War was replaced later by the necessary hard leather helmet. See also 'despatch rider'.

Motto Many regiments have their own personal motto which may appear as part of the badge, on the headdress or belt-plate. Cavalry regiments also used the sabretaches and shabraques as places to carry the motto. Drums and trumpet banners also often had the motto.

Mounted Rifles In the middle of the 19th century the American Mounted Rifles wore for a short time the badge of a perpendicular trumpet by both officers and men.

Mourning The signs of mourning in the British Army of the 18th century were elaborate. Buttons were covered with black crepe and black arm bands and sword-knots were also popular. In the next century pictures show drums covered with black crepe (no doubt also in earlier times) and also great swathes at the top of regimental colours. In modern time the Household Cavalry standards have been seen with mourning trimmings.

Mourning lace It has sometimes been said that the black line in officers' lace indicates mourning for a famous person or officer. Such a reason is hard to prove as in the case of the Gordon Highlanders who connect it with the death of Sir John Moore in 1809 but the black line had been worn years before that event. The black line for the 17th Light Dragoons was to commemorate the death of General Wolfe and this could be correct, as in the case of the officers of the Norfolk Regiment who introduced a black line in their lace in 1881 to commemorate Moore (although it should be mentioned that the men had black lines in their lace as early as 1768). See also Black line in lace.

Moustaches The British soldier often preferred to be clean-shaven but toward the end of the 18th century it was permissible

Motto. Metal badge with Scottish motto on circlet

Mullet. The Douglas mullet on badge of Scottish Rifles

Mural Crown. On badge of Prince Albert's Somerset Light Infantry

to grow side-whiskers and for certain musicians to have a moustache. Pioneers had been allowed full beards much earlier. The employment of foreign troops like the men of the 5th and 6th battalions of the 60th Foot saw moustaches in common wear. The conversion of light dragoons to hussars brought the hussars' thin moustache into the British Army as also happened when lancers were created in 1816. The Royal Horse Artillery whose uniform tended towards that of hussars also brought the moustache and even a full beard is known at the time of Waterloo. Grenadiers early in the 17th century had worn moustaches and the Royal Scots Greys being considered as a kind of mounted grenadier were wearing moustaches at Waterloo. But it was the rigorous winters in the Crimea that saw moustaches and beards worn commonly, and being kept by veterans when they returned home. According to the Queen's Regulations of 1885 the moustache was to be worn but the underlip and chin shaven. About 1923 the wearing of moustaches became optional.

MT The initials 'MT' in laurels on an arm badge denote proficiency in mechanical transport but the badge has long been obsolete.

Mufti An Urdu word meaning 'free' and indicates that civilian dress of a fixed pattern was issued free to the lower grades of soldier, for walking out or private use.

Mullet The heraldic mullet, a five-pointed star, appears in badges of the Cameronians, Scottish Rifles, as the mullet was in the coat-of-arms of the Lord Angus, house of Douglas, who raised the regiment in the 17th century.

Multani mutti An ochre dye used on the clothing of Indian native troops.

Mundir An officer's tunic in the Russian Czarist army.

Mural Crown This heraldic device is used in the badges of the 13th Foot, later the Somerset Light Infantry (still later the Somerset and Cornwall before being merged into the Light Infantry). The crown is patterned as a crenellated wall and signifies the defence of Jellalabad in 1842 against the Afghans.

Musicians As musicians were not fighting men, it has been the practice to dress them differently from the common soldier. The dress of bandsmen, drummers, fifers and pipers vary and should be seen under their own heading.

Musket As the musket was the common weapon of infantry, the badge of an embroidered musket or muskets was worn to show proficiency with that weapon. In the present century the word musket has been replaced by 'rifle', although the rifled musket was the earlier name to differentiate it from the smooth bore arm.

Musketry Skill in firing a musket or rifle was indicated by the wearing of such weapons as an arm badge, plus a crown, star, etc., to indicate the degree of proficiency whether as a prize badge or skill-at-arms. See also 'marksman', 'sniper', etc.

Musketeer Usually applies to the soldier of the 17th century who had a heavy musket with or without a rest and a bandolier of charges. When matchlocks went out of fashion and the pikeman became obsolete the common weapon was the musket and therefore no separate name was needed.

Mutze German, cap.

Nackenschrim German, back peak of a shako or headdress.

Napoleon boots Obviously a boot preferred by Napoleon. High black boots covering the knee in front but cut away behind.

Neckwear White cravats or neck cloths were worn in Charles II's reign. These could go twice about the neck and tie in front. The cloth was eventually worn as a stock with no ends showing. By 1743 the black stock was becoming popular as it did not dirty as quickly but red stocks are known, presumably to mark the difference between similarly dressed regiments. Officers are known to have had black velvet stocks and the men horsehair, but after the American Revolution the material changed to black leather. At the end of the 18th century it was found that in the heat of the West Indies black cloth was better for the men than leather. For a time both leather and cloth were worn but it then became the rule for other ranks to have leather. After being made pliant for a time, they had to be stiffened again. It was the Crimean War which saw stocks being discontinued and a leather tab was worn inside the collar instead. This changed to cloth and eventually disappeared.

In the 20th century the introduction of an open neck for officers' tunics brought about the use of collar and ties, a fashion permitted for other ranks in battle dress at the end of the Second World War. In hot climates when open-necked shirts were worn, the sweat-rag or cloth was again worn around the neck. Following the fashion of American troops, coloured cravats may be seen with combat dress. See also cravat, foxtails, stock and steenkirk.

Needle The point or aglet of an aiguillette.

Netted button Before the all-metal button came into use it was customary in the army to have a shape of wood or bone covered with thread or wire. The top of the 'pill-box' cap (with or without peak) had an ornament on top called a netted button. This was a button-shaped piece of wood covered with thread or wire for officers although the other ranks had cloth.

Nigger cloth Another term for the 'butternut' clothing worn by Confederate troops because it had been worn by slaves.

Nivernois In the third quarter of the 18th century the tricorn hat was made small and cocked into the 'Nivernois' fashion, named after the duke of that name, 1716–38. It was worn by dandies and European officers in India seemed to like it particularly.

No. 1 Dress With the abolition of full dress in the British Army, the orders of dress remaining were numbered in sequence after the naval fashion. The nearest to a ceremonial full dress was the No. 1 dress, the 'blues' (or green in the case of riflemen and others) but this gave place to service dress.

Numbers or numerals In the 18th and 19th centuries regiments

Needle. The metal points on an aiguillette

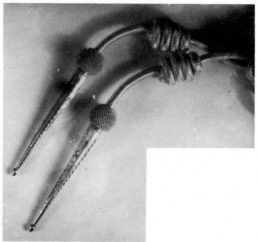

Number. '42' is the regimental number of the Black Watch or Royal Highlanders

of infantry were numbered in sequence and precedence and these numbers could appear on the equipment, belt-plates and head-dress. The introduction of the territorial system of 1881 saw the discontinuation of these numbers, although the number of a battalion might appear on the shoulder-strap. Militia regiments in the 19th century had their own sequence of numbering which differed from the regulars but these also disappeared in 1881. The volunteers of the 1860s onwards might have had the shire number of the corps or the sequence number but these were finished when the re-organisation brought volunteer battalions into the regimental battalion numbering. The London Regiment, created in 1908, had battalions which in theory were numbered up to 28. Cavalry of the Line also had their own numbering in the 18th and 19th century but disbandment and amalgamation make the modern numbering almost incomprehensible, and very few remain.

Oilskin cover. On shako, *c.*1868

O This letter within laurel sprays was the arm badge of a qualified observer from *c.*1915 until it was abolished in 1921. In the Second World War it may have been employed to designate an 'operator'. Combined with a crown and a wing it is the embroidered badge worn by a qualified observer in the Army Air Corps. An 'o' combined with flashes of lightning is the arm badge for an operator, Fire Control in the Royal Artillery from 1947–58. In many other colour combinations the circle and flashes indicate proficiency in specialists of radio and telecommunication.

Oakleaf The badge of an oakleaf was and is worn as an American rank badge; in gold for a major and in silver for a lieutenant-colonel.

Oakleaves A popular German idea was to wear oakleaves in the headdress after a battle. As the Hanoverian Kings of Britain were of German extraction the fashion for British troops to wear oakleaves on special occasions was popular in the 18th century.

The tradition of the English oaktree and its connection with Prince Charles's (later Charles II) escape in the Boscobel Oak is said to account for oakleaves on the helmets and in the embroidery of the Household Cavalry. They are also worn by field marshals and general officers in their lace and embroidery.

OCTU Officer Cadet Training Unit. These officer-producing units so popular in the Second World War covered all arms of service. After the war they were replaced by other established Officer Cadet centres. The uniforms were those of officers (without rank except any local appointment) and with distinctions of white. Discs were worn behind cap badges, in the case of the Royal Armoured Corps ivorine diamonds were worn. The cap f.s. had white inset patches of cloth in front and white cap bands were worn with the service dress cap. Strips of material on the shoulder-straps were sometimes worn.

Offizier–Kollet Besides the double-breasted *kollet* worn by German other ranks there was an officer pattern of finer cloth of which the collar and cuffs were velvet. Buttons were either gold or silver.

Oilskin cover The elaborate shakos of the 19th century were not all of leather but of velvet or felt on a pasteboard foundation. Thus in bad and wet weather the caps or shakos often went out of shape. It became the fashion to have a fitting oilskin cover to go over the cocked hat and shako from 1812 onwards. Unfortunately this produced a heavy headdress and at least one case is known of an officer cutting off the hidden golden bullions to make a lighter headdress. The Highland feather bonnet also became very heavy in the rain and also had a cover with ties as can be noted in the first

I.   On Napoleon's abdication, Louis XVIII revived the Maison du Roi and so in 1814 the Grey and the Black Musketeers were re-raised. The second company seen here rode black horses and wore dark blue *soubrevests* (p.122) with epaulettes (p.58).

II.   American infantry officer and sergeant in field dress in the Philippines, 1903, by H. Charles McBarron.

1. France. 1804–1810. Cuirassiers These uniforms
drawn by Lucien Rousselot show helmets of the 1st
Regiment (fig. 9) and the 9th Regiment (fig. 10)
differing in the pompon. The iron cuirass (fig. 11) has
brass or gilt fittings on a red lining (see cuirass, p. 45)
Fig. 16 shows a maréchal fourant of 1809 with the
badge of a red horseshoe on his arm (see horseshoe,
p. 73). Figures 14 and 18 wear the bonnet de police
(see p. 29).

2. France. 1750. Cavalérie These illustrations also by Lucien Rousselot show the heavy cavalry (fig. 14 and 20) wearing the front piece only of the cuirass. The tricorn hats (see p. 129) show three views of this complex headdress. The buff waist belts (fig. 8 and 20) have slings (see p. 121) for the long sword. The cloak (see p. 40) is ample enough to cover the equipment behind the saddle.

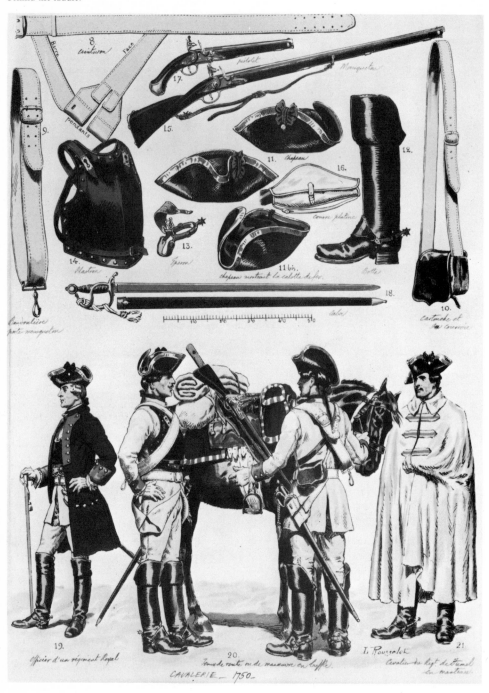

3. Great Britain. 1810. 19th Lancers A contemporary print by S. and J. Fuller shows the lancer dress as introduced to the British Army after Waterloo. The jacket (see p. 76) is blue with yellow facings, a colour also on the top of the schapska (see p. 115) or lance cap (see p. 82). The undress sabretache (see p. 114) is plain black without any device. Around the waist is a girdle (see p. 64) gold and crimson for officers, blue and yellow for the men. The shabraque (see p. 118) is blue with yellow edging.

LINIEN - INFANTERIE.

(1808.)

Grenadier. — Voltigeur.

Left **4. France. 1808. Line Infantry** This print by
L. Bellange shows on the left a grenadier (see p. 68)
with red epaulettes, plume and shako cords. On the
right the voltigeur or light infantryman has yellow
distinctions on the shako as well as green fringe on his
epaulettes. The lower part of his plume is also green.

5. France. *c.***1812** This plate from Goddard and Booth's
Military Costumes of Europe (1812) shows three soldiers.
On the left is a man of the Horse Artillery. His shako
(see p. 118) has a red plume and his short jacket (see
p. 76) is blue with red trimmings as are his breeches.
In the middle is a hussar of the 2nd or Chamborant
Hussars. His plume is light blue over brown. His
jacket and pelisse (see p. 100) are also brown with blue
cuffs and white trimmings. His breeches are also light
blue and he wears hessian boots (see p. 72). The figure
on the right is a cuirassier of the 6th Regiment with a
red plume to his helmet and a red lining to his cuirass.

6. Russia. 1807. Body Guard This and the accompanying print are from contemporary prints made in 1807 by Edward Orme when the Russians were allies fighting against Napoleon and the costume may be a trifle fanciful. The cuirassier wears his armour over a greencoat whereas the white garment is better known. His bicorn hat has a red plume and his nether wear is white breeches and high jack boots.

BODY GUARD

7. Russia. 1807. Infantry This dress has elements of an earlier period specially in the headdress. The man still wears his hair queued, a style going out of fashion at that date. His dark green coat has red facings (see p. 54) for the collar, cuffs, shoulder-straps and turnbacks. His black gaiters (see p. 62) button up to the knee.

INFANTRY.

8. Prussia. *c*.1786. Leib Regiment zu Pferd Nr. 3
Adolph Menzel produced a great work on the military uniforms of the army of Frederick the Great. The headdress is in the transition period from tricorn to bicorn (see Hat, p. 71) and the white plume has a black top for officers. The white koller has dark blue collar and cuffs with gold braid for officers. The sabretache (see p. 114) is fastened high on the right side, a distinction for heavy cavalry. The sword knot or faustriemen (see p. 55) is white arising from a blue base.

9. Prussia. *c.*1786. **Dragoon Regiment** These cavalrymen of Frederick the Great's era are drawn by Adolph Menzel. The blue coat with red facings is almost hidden under the ample light grey cloak (see p. 40). The black tip on the feather of the right-hand soldier, shows him to be an officer.

10. United States of America. 1781. Artillery and Infantry This plate, by H. Charles McBarron, shows an artilleryman guarding his cannon. His long lapels (see p. 83) are scarlet as are the other facings. He wears gaiter-trousers (see p. 62). The officer with the espontoon has a silver epaulette (see p. 53) on his left shoulder, to indicate that he is a subaltern. The buff facings were worn by both the New York and New Jersey infantry. The white and black rosette (see p. 111) on the hat indicate the Union with France.

11. United States of America. 1827. Artillery and Infantry By H. Charles McBarron showing the artillery officer with wings (see p. 137) which were worn for a short period as well as the gold rank chevrons on the upper arm. The infantry sergeant on the right has a red tuft (see p. 129) on his shako and white worsted rolls on his shoulders, both signs of the grenadier company. The drummers at the rear have red coats although the Artillery School troops have all blue coats or coatees.

12. United States of America. Engineers, Infantry and Artillery The Union Army by the American artist H. Charles McBarron. The engineer officer has a plain frock coat (see p. 60) with his red sash (see p. 114) under his waistbelt. His shoulder rank markings are single bars (see p. 23) to indicate a 1st lieutenant.

The advancing infantry 1st sergeant has rank chevrons of the infantry light blue as well as a red sash round the waist of his sack coat (see p. 114). The red acorn on top of his kepi indicates the 1st Division of the 14th Army Corps.

13. United States of America. 1918. Artillery officer and machinegun sergeant The Americans entered the First World War complete with steel helmets (see p. 124) of the British pattern. The drab tunic of the officer has a closed collar – the British had an open neck with collar and tie, and his pistol holster is on a web belt (see webbing, p. 135). The machinegun sergeant has a painted divisional sign on his helmet, that of the ivy-leaves, representing 'IV' for the 4th Division. He wears putties (see p. 106) as the normal canvas leggings were in short supply.

Left **14. Great Britain. *c*.1812. Infantry officers**
From Goddard and Booth's Military Costume of
Europe, come two hand-coloured engravings. On the
left is an officer of the 87th or Prince of Wales's Own
Irish Regiment wearing the new headdress introduced
in 1812 and later known as the Waterloo shako. His
scarlet jacket (see p. 76) has the lapels buttoned across
to show the black facings. At his neck he has a gilt
gorget (see p. 66). On the right is an officer of the
25th Foot or King's Own Borderers. His scarlet coat is
only partly buttoned over and allows the turned down
lapels to show the dark blue facings. He still wears the
bicorn hat (see p. 26) which on service was superseded
by the new pattern shako. His curved sword has a
mameluke hilt (see p. 88)

Above **16. 1869. Great Britain. Infantry of the Line**
This group is from a lithograph by G. H. Thomas and
is numbered '6' in a series. On the left is a bandsman in
his white jacket (see p. 76) and next to him is a
drummer in a red tunic with distinctive drummers'
braid or lace (see p. 82). Next is an infantry private in
red and then a man from the Rifle Brigade in green.
The pioneer has his axe over his shoulder and sports a
full beard – a privilege of that trade. The sergeant of
light infantry has a green falling plume instead of the
round ball tuft worn by others. The Highland piper
wears a green doublet (see p. 48) and a six-tailed
sporran (see p. 122). The corporal of the 78th
Highlanders has a shoulder or fly plaid (see p. 103).

15. Great Britain. 1854. Scots Fusilier Guards This fine print by G. H. Thomas shows these soldiers (now the Scots Guards) cheering Queen Victoria before departing for the Crimean War. The officer in front wears his dark blue frock coat (see p. 60) and waves his forage cap (see p. 59) which has a diced border (see p. 47). The guardsmen raise their bearskin caps (see p. 25) and wear the coatee (see p. 40) which was soon changed for the tunic (see p. 130). The turnbacks of their coatees have ornaments (see p. 97) of the St Andrew thistle star (see p. 127)

17. Great Britain. 1856. 17th Lancers Queen Victoria was proud of her veterans of the Crimean War and invited the men of the 17th Lancers to Windsor Castle to be photographed by Robert Howlett, who took several group photographs of them. The loose double-breasted tunic (see p. 130) was introduced during the war and has the distinctive regimental white collar and piping. The lance-cap (see p. 82) has a white top and the plate in front the skull and cross-bones (see p. 121) of the regiment. The double white stripes on the overalls denote light cavalry.

18. Great Britain. *c.*1890. **Seaforth Highlanders**
This late Victorian photograph shows a corporal
standing by the kit laid out on his bed for inspection.
He wears a drill jacket (see p. 49) and tartan trews
(see p. 129) with white spats (see p. 122) just visible
below. His feather bonnet (see p. 29) is high on a shelf
for safety and his sporran (see p. 122) is below. The
glengarry (see p. 65) with its diced border (see p. 47)
is just in front of the sporran. Folded on the bed is his
doublet (see p. 48), the gauntlet cuffs (see p. 63) of
which are quite prominent.

19. India. *c.*1865. **19th Bengal Lancers** This exotic
group shows officers and men of the 19th Bengal
Lancers (Fane's Horse) sheltering under a tent at Mian
Mir. The British officers wear forage caps (see p. 59)
and either frocks or shell jackets. The native officers
wear turbans (see p. 130) and blouses or 'kurthas'. All
favour the native cummerbund (see p. 46) with
elaborately embroidered ends. Standing at the back on
the right are the non-commissioned officers with more
simple garments but most will be seen wearing medals
for China and elsewhere.

20. **India. 1886. 11th Bengal Lancers** Photographs were taken by Johnson and Hoffman when Indian troops were visiting Great Britain. This cavalry man has a red pag just showing under his turban (see p. 130) which has blue stripes on a white ground. His blue garment has a plain red cummerbund and his high jack boots are much in the style of the Household Cavalry.

21. India. 1886. 3rd Ghurka Rifles This is another posed photograph by Johnston and Hoffman – the apparatus for keeping the soldier still may be seen in the ground but the metal holder for the neck cannot be observed. The small cap is one of the many versions of the Kilmarnock (see p. 78) and the badge of the crossed kukris (see p. 81) included the regiment number. The dark green tunic is distinctive in having three-pointed flaps on the cuffs. Black leather gaiters (see p. 62) were also worn in the British Army at this period.

22. Australia. 1899. Victoria Mounted Rifles This sergeant major poses with the regimental mascot, a wallaby or small kangaroo. He wears an early version of the bush hat (see p. 33) which has a plaited pugri which was intended to combat the heat. The fashion of wearing khaki (see p. 78) or service drab (see p. 48) clothing was relieved with the addition of collar and cuffs in red cloth, as worn by Victorian forces at this time. He wears brown leather gloves and the Sam Browne belt for the sword was now almost of universal usage. The breeches are of a corduroy material capable of long wear.

23. Great Britain. 1901. Argyll and Sutherland Highlanders This photograph shows all the aspects of the elaborate Scottish uniform. The heavy tails and feathers of the bonnet (see p. 29) hide the distinctive red and white dicing of this regiment. The doublet (see p. 48) has the striking buttons and loops on the skirt flaps and gauntlet cuffs (see p. 63). The shoulder plaid (see p. 103) is held on the left shoulder by a circular brooch (see p. 31). The sporran has six bells and tassels (see p. 122), and a complete badger's head. The diced hose (see p. 73) are kept up by scarlet garter flashes (see p. 63) and on the second officer from the left, the top of his skein dhu (see p. 118) is just visible above his right hose top. The gaiters in this regiment have white buttons although black were worn elsewhere.

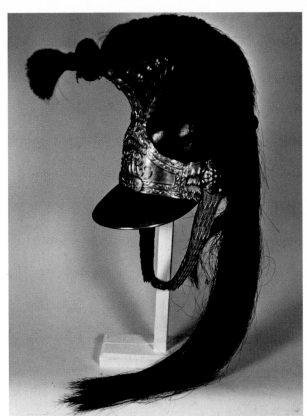

III. The 6th Dragoon Guards helmet (p.72) is dated 1834-43. The lion finial could be changed for a fur crest (p.44). Chin-scales (p.39) were worn at this time.

IV. The helmet of the 4th Dragoon Guards has a leather skull and horse-hair plume on the gilt crest (p.44) as worn from 1812 to 1818.

V. This shako (p.118) of the 2nd Royal Bucks Yeomanry was worn about 1840. It has silver lace (p.82) around the top to denote an officer. A chin-chain (p.39) was worn as well as a boss (p.30) in front.

VI. This officer's shapska (p.115) was worn by the 17th Lancers *c*.1838. It has the skull and cross bones device (p.121) in front and lion-headed ear-bosses (p.52).

VII.   In 1742 the Scots Greys were known as the Royal Regiment of Dragoons of North Britain. They wore grenadier caps (p.68), gauntlets (p.63) and a large pouch (p.104) which could hold grenades.

VIII.   A. Menzel reconstructed the uniform of a trumpeter of the Prussian Kurassier Regiment Nr. 2 of Frederick the Great's period. His cocked hat (p.41) has a standing feather (p.53) as well as feather round the brim.

IX.   This group of British infantry c.1869 shows a bandsman (p.22), a drummer (p.50), and further along a pioneer (p.102), a sergeant of light infantry (p.85), a Highland piper (p.102) and a Highland soldier (p.72).

Ornament. 'Crowsfoot' or 'bow' on skirt ornaments, *c.*1800

Outward Bound. The embroidered arm badge for the 'silver' award of the Outward Bound School

half of the 19th century. See also 'foul weather headdress'.

Olivet These thread-covered shapes or moulds (usually of wood) were worn by hussars on pelisse, stable jacket or frock coat. Being of various shapes (round, billet, etc.) these olivets served as buttons in the original Hungarian dresses.

Opanker, opanky Openwork peasant footwear worn by Balkan troops, including the Serbians in the First World War.

Orders of Dress There was originally only one dress for the common soldier, but the introduction of undress, fatigue dress, walking-out dress, tropical dress and so on brought about after the Second World War, a numbered order of dress (following the naval fashion for rigs) ranging from ceremonial order of dress down to shirt sleeve order. The changes of fashion have altered the uniforms and their numbered sequence in a few years. See also 'No. 1 dress'.

Ornament Although most decorative parts of uniform appear ornamental and are called 'ornaments', most parts began in a practical manner. For example the patches on the back of a coatee indicate where pocket flaps once existed. The elaborate embroidered ornaments on the skirts of coatees mark the place where strengtheners were placed to keep the skirt linings turned back. The elaborate 'slashes' on the cuffs of the Foot Guards mark the place where the large cuff turned up and was fastened in place.

Outward Bound The Army Outward Bound School encourages young soldiers to achieve certain feats of endurance and self-reliance. Participants receive three categories of award – 'A' the Gold, 'B' the Silver and 'C' the Bronze. The elaborate embroidered badges are in coloured silks with the coloured letters.

Overalls Military overalls were intended to go over breeches and gaiters, although loose trousers had been worn at the end of the 18th century. The General Order of 29 August 1811 authorised grey trousers and gaiters for troops in the Peninsula. In January 1812 infantry on service were permitted to wear overalls of unbleached linen on marches or light duties. About the same time all cavalry on service were permitted grey overalls with strapping. When breeches and gaiters became obsolete for full dress in 1823, the term 'trousers' became common for infantry but overalls continued in use for cavalry, referring to the close-fitting garments strapped under the instep.

Overcoat For most of the 17th and 18th centuries the soldier's coat was considered sufficient protection against the bad weather, although the use of sentry-gowns and watchcoats was extended for night duty although in short supply. But by the end of the 18th century the coat was cut down to follow fashion and the need for an overcoat for infantry was realised. In 1792 a Royal Warrant provided watchcoats for men on sentry duty and in 1801 an improved pattern of 'pepper and salt' led the way to the greatcoat which was issued in 1811. A new pattern was produced in 1829 but grey continued to be the infantry colour while full dress

97

remained in use. When khaki was introduced the overcoat also became khaki or service drab. The Foot Guards however continue to wear grey overcoats; Atholl grey being the shade for officers.

Overseas cap The American undress cap became popular in the First World War when this khaki 'fore-and-aft' cap was somewhat similar to the cap f.s. of the British Army. Now called the garrison cap it is made in different materials for units and overseas service.

Osnabruk, Osnaburg A coarse linen used for lining coats and garments, taking its name from Osnabrück in Prussia where it was first made.

P This letter in a wreath is the arm badge for a qualified plotter in a Fortress Plotting room of the Royal Artillery. Introduced in 1939 it appears to have lapsed in 1956.

Pack The receptacle in which soldiers' possessions are packed. The haversac, valise and knapsack might be considered as packs but the use of the word here seems unofficial as employed in 'pack-drill'. From the mid-19th century onwards the word 'pack' has come to mean a single item and in the modern equipment the word pack is applied to the container. See knapsack, etc.

Pad See spine pad.

Pag, pug Cloth tied over the head under the turban by Hindus.

Pagri See 'pugri'.

Paletot French, also German, a double-breasted coat cut in tunic style. In blue or khaki worn by French Colonial infantry and artillery.

Pantaloon Originally a nether garment of breeches and stockings in one piece popularised by the Italian clown, Pantaloon. Now shortened to pants. Worn in the army as close-fitting breeches going all the way down to the ankles. White pantaloons with short gaiters are shown on many prints of Rowlandson's Volunteers just before the end of the 18th century. The 5th battalion of the 60th Foot wore blue pantaloons, no doubt as a more serviceable colour. Blue pantaloons made of stockingette were popular with the Royal Artillery and light cavalrymen. Some regiments of hussars adopted scarlet pantaloons for full dress although by the time of the Crimean War they were out of fashion. Pantaloons continued in wear but were of cloth, Berlin diagonal weave, which Queen Victoria approved for levées and evening wear.

Papachka Russian, the fur cap of the Cossacks, the taller version giving place to the flattened type as worn before the First World War.

Parachute The embroidered badge of a parachute worn on the arm denotes a qualified parachute jumper, as in ACI 1274 of 1942. Members of parachute units wear the badge of a parachute with wings but others not attached only wear the plain parachute. See also APJI.

Paradeanzug German, for parade dress.

Paris velvet This material was used to cover shakos as in the case of light dragoons just after the Crimean War.

Parka The original parka was a skin smock with an attached hood worn by Eskimos. A version of the parka has been worn by soldiers in modern times but the material is now of nylon or synthetic fibre.

Partisan, partizan A staved weapon with a broad blade pointed

Parachute. The embroidered arm badge of a qualified parachutist

at the top and with cutting edges on both sides. In the early 17th century partisans were carried by captains and lieutenants as a sign of rank. Continued in use at the Restoration but late in the reign of Charles II only the lieutenant carried the partisan. In 1684 partisans of lieutenants were to be returned to the Ordnance Office but they are said to have been again in use from 1688 to 1710. Still carried by Yeomen of the Guards as a ceremonial weapon.

Passenten German, epaulette-holder or strap.

Passgürtel German, cloth girdle worn by Uhlans.

Patches Name given to the laced or embroidered pieces on either side of the collar, vestiges of where the collar once buttoned down. See also 'gorget patches'.

Patrol jacket Early in 1867 the wearing of the patrol jacket was authorised by a General Order. The 1874 Dress Regulations specified it as being of blue cloth, 28 inches long from the bottom of the collar behind, for an officer five feet nine inches in height with a proportionate variation for any difference in height, rounded in front and edged with inch black mohair braid all round and up the openings at the side. On the front four double drop-loops, netted olivets and pockets with flaps, hook and eye fastening in front. The use of patrol jackets (instead of blue frock coats) for cavalry regiments is noted in the 1883 Dress Regulations. The variations of astrakhan fur trimmings are shown in the illustrated 1900 Dress Regulations.

Patrontache German, cartridge pouch.

Pattens These wooden clogs which raised the wearer above the poor roads might be considered civilian dress, but the Life Guards of Charles II when on duty outside the palace 'would relieve their gards in pattens' according to a contemporary writer. (Wood's *Life and Times*, 1663.)

Pattés d'épaule French, shoulder-straps.

Peak The military peak is also known as a shade. Not only on a cap (as opposed to a hat) but on other military headdresses. It is not always an eye-shade but in the case of the Albert shako it is also a neckshade.

Pelisse At the time of the American Revolution some regiments of British Light Dragoons took to wearing their upper jackets (also called 'kitts') slung from the shoulder like a pelisse. The 16th Light Dragoons for a time had permission to line their jackets with leopardskin but this was withdrawn in 1788. The employment of emigré corps in Great Britain saw the pelisse in popular use. At the turn of the century not only the light dragoons but the newly formed hussars wore the pelisse. The fur-lined pelisse was expected to be the winter 'overcoat' for hussars but was discontinued during the Crimean War when the tunic came into wear. Yeomanry regiments like the Royal Buckinghamshire Hussars and the Royal Gloucestershire Hussars who wore the short jacket also wore pelisses.

The original pelisse is said to have come from the wolfskin worn

Pelisse. The hanging over-garment of hussars

by the Hungarian light cavalrymen who killed these predators in the 17th century when they attacked the flocks and herds.

Pelz German for pelisse referring to the fur pelt.

Pelzmütze German, fur cap or busby worn by German hussars.

Percussion cap These small copper caps which fit over the firing pin of the percussion lock were kept in a small pouch in the right side of the waistbelt but some tunics or upper garments had a slit in this place for a small pocket to hold the caps.

Petticoat breeches Also known as Rhinegrave breeches, were popular civilian wear in the mid-17th century and in Charles II's army, the Foot Guards wearing them to be in the height of fashion for uniform was not quite developed at this date.

Pferdeausrustung German, saddlery.

Philabeg Scots, little kilt, see 'feile beg'.

Physical Training The badge for soldiers qualified in physical training portrays crossed swords even though swordsmanship is no longer necessary. The badge for the Army Physical Training Corps is a crown over crossed swords.

Pickelhaube German, nickname for the spiked helmet. Derived originally from *Becken haube* (the mediaeval basinet) through *beckel, bickel* and finally *pickel*.

Pickers These are the ornaments on chains fixed to a shoulder-belt. Originally these pointed pieces of metal were used to clean out the touch-hole of a pistol or carbine. When the flintlock went out of use, there was no further need for these pickers or prickers but cavalry officers retained them as ornaments. The common infantryman usually had a piece of wire and a rudimentary brush hanging from his crossbelt for the purpose of cleaning the lock.

Pigtail This name was given to the 'tail' of hair bound with tape at the back of the head in the 18th and 19th centuries. Hollow tubes of metal were also bound on to give the impression of greater length but in 1806 the soldiers' hair was officially cut short and worn in a normal fashion.

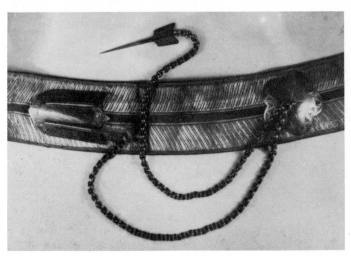

Pickers. The chains and pickers on light cavalry shoulder-belt

Pioneer. Northumberland Fusiliers, c.1872

Pike The weapon for a pikeman was originally 16 feet long, but later pikemen cut them down to 14 feet to make them less cumbersome in battle. Although replaced by the increase of muskets in a regiment by 1702 they were still carried ceremonially as late as 1705. The half pike was carried by officers in the late 17th century. The spontoon carried by sergeants from 1792 until 1830 might be considered a pike although it had a cross-bar.

Pikeman As pikemen were slow-moving and often had to be static to use their pikes to the best advantage, defences in the form of armour were needed. Backs, breasts and tasses were needed for the body although the tasses went out of fashion by Charles II's reign. The pikeman's helmet or 'pot' needed in battle was replaced by a hat in peacetime and on occasions when the helmet was carried behind at the waist. Waist sashes were worn by pikemen but as the weapon went out of fashion, armour ceased to be worn, the hat instead of the 'pot', the leather coat instead of the cuirass. By 1702 the pike was obsolete.

Pincers, pinchers This two-piece gripping tool is combined with a hammer to form the badge for artificers. See 'hammer' and 'pincers'.

Pioneer Labourers (*peone* in Spanish) were necessary on the field of battle for many tasks and each company of infantry was allocated at least one. When drawn up for inspection it was usual for all the pioneers to be on the right side and also to march in front of the regiment. They wore full beards or heavy moustaches as well as fur caps. The carrying of axes and the wearing of leather aprons indicated their trade. In fact these traditional items may still be seen in certain regiments today.

In the First World War battalions of pioneers were formed and wore special collar badges of crossed pickaxe and rifle. Qualified regimental pioneers are permitted to wear an arm badge of crossed axes or hatchets (q.v.). In the case of the Grenadier Guards, an embroidered grenade is worn above the axes, in the Coldstream Guards a rose, in the Scots Guards the Star of St Andrew and in the Irish Guards the Star of St Patrick. Light infantry regiments have the badge of a bugle, above their axes. Rifle regiments have black embroidered axes on dark green or scarlet. Fusiliers have the addition of a grenade. The section is known today as 'assault pioneers' and as such have 'offensive' tasks to undertake as well as defensive.

Piper Although captains of Highland companies had their own pipers, the dress as worn today did not emerge until the 19th century. Although military pipers date back to the 17th century, for a long time they wore the normal soldier's dress. In the second quarter of the 19th century pipers began to wear a tartan uniform but in 1856 most Highland regiments adopted the green doublet as worn today. Blue doublets were later worn as in the case of the Scots Guards. In 1881 Lowland regiments were allowed to wear the doublet. Glengarries were the full dress headdress of pipers.

Plaid. Worn by officer of 72nd Seaforth Highlanders, c.1870

Plume. Feather plume worn by officer of 17th Lancers, c.1830

Irish units have been slow to acquire pipers with a regimental uniform. The Tyrone Fusiliers (a militia battalion of the Royal Inniskilling Fusiliers) appear to have been the first to adopt pipers although others followed soon after. The Irish pipers' dress includes a caubeen, doublet, kilt and shawl of saffron colour as well as other varying distinctions. See also 'bagpiper'.

Piper green This is the colour of jackets worn by Highland regiments for the No. 1 Dress.

Pipe-major As a 'pipe-sergeant-major' this soldier wears a more elaborate version of the piper's dress usually with gold or silver decorations as well as rank distinctions. This applies equally to Scottish and Irish pipe bands.

Pistol Although not a badge in the British Army, the American Military Police have a pair of crossed pistols as a badge.

Pith helmet An Indian topee or sun helmet made from the pith of spongewood trees. Also called a cork helmet in 1861. See also 'Solar helmet'.

Plaid Worn by Highland soldiers made of regimental or traditional tartan. The Irish piper's equivalent is known as a shawl.

Plait (a) The hair on a soldier's head in the 18th century could either be in a queue or a plait – usually the distinction of grenadiers. (b) The plait could also refer to the plaited cord as on a grenadier's fur cap or even the plaited lanyard worn on the arm in modern times.

Plastron From the Italian, piastra meaning a breastplate. On uniform the broad piece of material placed on the chest and attached by two rows of buttons as in the case of lancers, light dragoons and some infantry.

Plate There are many varieties of plate in the army, normally meaning a flattish piece of metal. The lower front of the grenadier's fur cap had a distinguishing metal plate. Shakos and helmets had their plates as did shoulder and waist belts. See also under separate headings.

Plate (metal) Buttons of plate in the 17th and 18th century referred to buttons made of flat silver as opposed to gilt.

Plume Originally a feather decoration on a headdress but also applicable to hair plumes or even whalebone plumes. Plumes were worn extensively on helmets, on the brims of hats in the 17th and 18th centuries specially by officers. Light cavalry wore plumes of hair and later cut feathers. When infantry officers wore hackles or cut-feather plumes, the soldiers usually had worsted tufts.

Point The end of tags or ribbons had points or 'needles'.

Poke The projecting front of a hat or cap, a type of peak.

Polakem A Russian cloth cap with flaps to let down to cover ears and neck.

Polish cuff The Polish cuff came to a point towards the front.

Polrock From 'pol' for Polish and 'rock' German for coat – a German long-skirted frock-coat with hussar braiding.

Pompadour A delicate shade of purple, magenta, pink or grape according to various writings being the facing colour of the 56th and the 59th Regiments of Foot after the favourite colour of Madame Pompadour. Later, the Essex Regiment took the nickname of the 'Pompadours'.

Pompon French, for woollen tuft worn in shako of various colours and shapes by many nations. In the United States *c.*1825 infantry wore a white pompon, rifles green, cavalry yellow, light infantry white and red. Various other colours were also worn with the shako or cap.

Poncho A square of cloth with a hole in the centre as an opening for the head with the remainder acting as a protection against the bad weather and worn in the American and other armies.

Popinjay An 18th century term for a shade of green used as a facing colour and reminiscent of the popinjay or parrot.

Portepée French, sword-knot, capable of holding the sword suspended from the wrist.

Poshteen Indian native coat of sheepskin worn with the hair inside.

Pot Slang name for the helmet at the end of the 17th century.

Potemkin uniform Russian uniform introduced in December 1786 by Prince Potemkin. It includes a short jacket (*kurtka*), loose trousers and an unusual headdress with flaps which could protect the neck and ears.

Pouch The first grenadiers of the 17th century had large pouches on slings to hold their grenades. When the combined charges of the cartridge superseded the powder-horn system, pouches for the made-up cartridges gave protection in wet weather. Later, officers on horseback needed pouches on the shoulder-belt to hold the ammunition for their pistols and these continue in wear as ornaments to the present day.

Pouch-belt The pouch-belt (rather than the bayonet-belt and the cartridge-belt) became a mark of an officer and often was of gold or silver lace on a leather backing. Belts of plain black leather

Pouch. Officer, Life Guards, *c.*1815

were also worn, particularly by rifle officers. On the front cavalry officers had two small pickers on chain in order to clear the touch-holes of their pistols, a need which disappeared when the percussion cap and the revolver came in use.

Pouch-belt plate Rifle officers wore a pouch-belt in imitation of light cavalry officers and the front of these belts served to carry a complex badge with regimental honours and distinctions (which in normal infantry regiments appeared on the colours but which the rifle corps did not have).

Poukamiso Greek, the evzone shirt.

PPR These initials appeared on the uniform of the Paid-Pensioner-Recruiter 1924 to about 1933 when the title was changed to Army Recruiter and crossed flags were worn.

Priming horn A small horn containing fine gunpowder to prime the pan if matchlock or the flintlock, usually carried on a cord.

Prize badge In the second half of the 19th century soldiers were awarded prize badges for proficiency in musketry, artillery, lance drill, etc. See under separate headings.

Proficiency badges Special arm badges were introduced when proficiency in various trades and accomplishments was needed (and after prize badges were discontinued). All volunteers and militia were expected to earn general proficiency badges.

Propeller The device of a propeller as an arm badge in the army indicates proficiency in the RASC/RCT fleet (q.v.).

Prussian collar This was a stand-up collar which closed all the way up and not just at the bottom which gradually came into use in the British Army about 1820. It also encouraged an erect posture by the soldier.

Prussian Eagle As may be expected the eagle was a badge of the Prussian and later the German troops. It is also the badge of the 14th/20th Hussars, originally granted to the 14th Light Dragoons.

PT Abbreviation for Physical training, q.v.

Pouch-belt. Officer, 11th Hussars, late Victorian

Pugri, puggari, pagri Cloth wound around the head or head-dress (*kullah, pag* or helmet) in India.

Purse The Scottish sporran.

Puschel German, shako-tuft or ornament.

Puttees, putties Cloth wound around the legs to cover the top of boots and prevent mud and dust entering. Introduced in the late 19th century. Both in long and short version. Originally cotton but later made of wool.

Pyjamas, paijamas Loose trousers worn by Indian cavalrymen.

QI. Arm badge of Qualified Instructor of Royal Engineers

QI Qualified instructors of artillery, engineers, physical training, signals, weapons, horse riding and parachuting, all have their own special badge (q.v.).

Quasten German, hanging knots or tassels, of sword or bayonet knot.

Queen's Crown This term usually refers to the crown used as a badge in Queen Victoria's reign, which gave place in 1901 to the 'King's crown', more properly the Tudor crown.

Queue The hair gathered at the back of the head in the late 18th century and tied in a long tail. See also 'flash'.

Quilted cover In order to counter-act the heat, and the sun's rays, white quilted covers were added to the military headdresses in India in the 19th century.

Quilted shako The infantry shako in use 1861 to 1869 had a stitched body copied from the French Army.

Quartermaster Four chevrons were introduced in 1802 to indicate the rank of quartermaster-sergeant. These were worn point downwards on the upper right arm. In 1869 they were worn below the elbow still point down. In 1881 they were worn point upwards. A regimental quartermaster sergeant wore in addition an eight-pointed star until the First World War. During that war the grades of senior NCOs were re-organised and the Warrant Officer grouping had new badges of rank. The crown and wreath (or the crown and three chevrons for squadron quartermaster) with other service differences came in use.

Racoon cap. Worn by Fusiliers, *c*.1904

R (a) The letter 'R' on the shoulder-strap of an officer indicated Reserve; (b) with laurel sprays is worn as an arm badge by a Range taker, a class introduced about 1914; (c) with flashes worn on the arm by radar technicians in the Royal Electrical and Mechanical Engineers.

Rabatten German, the plastron of a lancer's tunic.

Racoon Although it was usual in the early days to issue grenadiers and fusiliers with bearskin caps, in the 1870s racoonskin caps were regulation for fusilier regiments. The 1874 Dress Regulations quotes black racoonskin caps as being nine inches high but the 1900 Dress Regulations states either bearskin or racoon, which alternative continued until the end of full dress.

Radar Those men qualified in Radar (fire control) were permitted in 1965 this word in laurel sprays as an arm badge.

Raggie In the first part of the 19th century a single-breasted undress garment which could be worn as a pelisse was adopted by some mounted men.

Ranger A ranger is a soldier who 'ranges' the countryside to fight the enemy instead of fighting in serried ranks. Thus the men in groups like Roger's Rangers and the Queen's Rangers have a green (or colour other than red) uniform to act as camouflage.

Rank Badges of rank should be readily visible marks on uniform to see the degree of rank of the wearer. See under 'crown', 'star', 'chevrons', 'royal arms', etc. The Indian Army in the late 18th century began a system of rank markings for officers but it was not until February 1810 that the British Army authorised such a system. For infantry regiments the colonel wore two epaulettes each with a crown and star, the lieutenant-colonel epaulettes with a crown and the major epaulettes and a star. A captain had a single

Rank badges. Various embroidered types

epaulette on the right shoulder and lieutenants the epaulette with a thinner fringe. The introduction of the tunic instead of the coatee in 1855 continued the same marking but on the collar as epaulettes were obsolete. For field officers the collar was laced all round. The three junior ranks had lace or braid on the top and front of the collar only, with the captain now wearing a crown and star, the lieutenant a crown and the ensign (changed to 2nd lieutenant in 1876) a star. In October 1880 rank was again worn on the shoulder, this time on twisted cords with a change of badges. The colonel had a crown and two stars, the lieutenant-colonel a crown and star, the major a crown, the captain two stars, the 1st lieutenant one star and the 2nd (or sub-) lieutenant no device. In May 1902 the 2nd lieutenant was granted a star, a lieutenant two and a captain three.

Raquette French, a plaited shape at the end of headdress cords, above the final tassel.

Rattan An Indian palm from which regiments found the material for the insides of sun helmets.

RASC/RCT Fleet The Army Service Corps, later the Royal Corps of Transport, employed small boats for Inland Water Transport and for port work with the army. In recent years personnel were given badges to indicate their nautical prowess. On discs of yellow cloth one and a half inches wide were embroidered badges of a ship's wheel, a propeller or a knot. Since 1968 the Royal Corps of Transport has had new arm badges, an anchor on purple for a Chief Engineer and an anchor on ultramarine for an Ocean Watch Keeper.

Raupenhelme German, a helmet with a worsted (or other soft material) crest reminiscent of a caterpillar.

Ravenduck A type of canvas used in the second half of the 18th century to make jackets, waistcoats and trousers for fatigue purposes.

Reamer A tool for enlarging holes in cannon, part of the equipment worn on the shoulder-belt of artillery men in the 18th century.

Recruiter Recruiting staff in the 19th century wore red, white and blue ribbons in the headdress to indicate their work. In the 20th century the recruiters were a separate branch and wore an embroidered badge of crossed Union flags. See also 'PPR'.

Red Cross This device is not only carried on medical vehicles but was worn by qualified personnel as an arm badge. See 'Geneva Cross'.

Redingote French version of a riding coat of cavalrymen, a greatcoat with wide skirts to spread over the horse.

Reitstiefel German, riding boots.

Respirator A device for filtering air during a gas attack. See also 'gas mask'.

Rest A staff with a metal finial in which to rest the musket. Carried by musketeers in the days when the musket was too heavy

RASC/RCT Fleet. Embroidered arm badge of flag of Army Fleet

and needed a free hand for firing.

Reversed colours It was customary to reverse the colours of the coat and the facings in the case of drummers and similar musicians from the late 17th century onwards. Thus the green cuff seen on a fighting man would become the green coat of a drummer in his regiment. In Royal regiments like the Foot Guards this reversal was not necessary as the national scarlet retained the royal blue for all ranks. See also 'facings', 'drummer', etc.

Reversed cypher The initials of a commander, royal, noble and even non-royal were combined to form a reversible pattern called a cypher, often including extra reversed letters so that the two sides were similar. The cypher was carried on the front of the drum, on cloth caps of grenadiers and on the coat of musicians. Later in the 18th century these reversed cyphers went out of fashion. See also 'cypher'.

Ribband In the early months of the American Revolution senior officers were distinguished by the ribband or sash worn over the shoulder. Washington as commander-in-chief had one of light blue, major-generals at first pink then purple, brigadier-generals pink and aides-de-camp green.

Riding instructor As a distinction of the uniform of such a man an arm badge of an embroidered spur was worn from at least 1877 onwards.

Rifle A badge containing a rifle (or musket) normally indicated proficiency in that weapon by the wearer. Embroidered crossed muskets in 1864 showed skill-at-arms for a marksman. Single rifles also indicated marksmanship in the cadet forces. At first worn on the left arm with the barrel to the front, and pointing to the left, the direction changed when a new type of brassard was worn on the right arm only. See 'crossed muskets', etc.

Rifle green This colour favoured by huntsmen (*jägers* in German and *chasseurs* in French) was worn by riflemen in the 18th century and by the King's Royal Rifle Corps and the Rifle Brigade. The shade of green was quite deep but not as dark as invisible green (q.v.).

Ringkragen German, gorget.

Rock German, coat.

Rod and serpent This badge within a wreath is the modern badge for a qualified 1st Aid instructor.

Roman helmet This term was applied officially to the metal crested helmet worn by the Household Cavalry and heavy cavalry from *c*.1817 until it was replaced by the Albert helmet (q.v.) *c*.1842. The term was not strictly accurate and some considered the helmet to be Grecian in design.

Rose The floral emblem of England, the rose frequently appears on uniforms as well as on regimental colours or drums. The Royal Fusiliers in late 17th century days had the rose on the cloth grenadier caps and elsewhere. Yorkshire, Lancashire and Hampshire units all have badges of their own county design for infantry

Rose. Embroidered silver rose of Coldstream Guards

or yeomanry. The Coldstream Guards also have the embroidered rose as an arm badge worn in conjunction with the crossed hatchets of pioneers and also on the shoulder-straps of rank and file.

Rose (helmet) Many British cavalry helmets of recent years have metal boss with the pattern of a rose.

Rose lace When infantry officers' lace was simplified in 1881, a rose pattern lace was chosen for the English (and Welsh) regiments.

Rosette A pleated round shape on a headdress (shako or Highland bonnet) originally made of ribbons or cloth but also imitated in leather or metal. Rosettes were also worn at the back of the head when hair was queued in the 18th century.

Rosshaarschweif German, horsehair tail on a headdress.

Rough rider In the late 19th century the Rough Rider of cavalry wore the badge of a spur on his arm. In 1881 the Royal Artillery also adopted the badge but wore it on red cloth. In 1923 'rough riders' were replaced by riding instructors who continued to wear the spur badge.

Round cord This cord was a tubular lace of gold or silver wire over a core of cotton or other material and worn by the Royal Horse Artillery and Hussars on their jackets.

Round hats The round hat was a civilian headdress but worn much by military men when serving abroad. In 1776 5000 round hats were sent to America. After the end of the War of Independence the white round hat was worn extensively in India both for infantry and artillerymen. In 1791 the black round hat was ordered not to be less than six inches high with a false lining. This made a space above the head to keep the heat at a minimum and the all round brim served to protect the eyes from the sun. The expedition to the Netherlands in 1793 and to Egypt in 1799 saw the round hat being worn by most soldiers. It was to be seen in Surinam in 1800 and infantry officers in the Isle of Wight waiting to proceed on overseas service had the hat with a small feather. The Royal Marines continued to wear the round hat after Waterloo.

Royal Arms The royal coat-of-arms appeared on gorgets changing with the monarchs until 1796 when the royal cypher was used instead. In fact the Regiments of Foot Guards (being the king's own troops) continued to display the arms on their gorgets. The Royal Artillery was authorised a shako plate in 1833 which had the royal arms and it continued to be worn when the helmet came in. Household cavalry helmets from 1817 to 1832 had the royal arms on the front plate as did heavy cavalry from 1818 to 1847. The front plate on lance caps also had the royal arms. The Royal Scots Fusiliers put the royal arms on their grenade badge and other soldiers such as those in the General List wore a badge with the full coat-of-arms in the First World War.

As a badge of rank, a small royal arms was worn in 1915 for Warrant Officers Class 1 as were the royal arms within a wreath.

Royal Army Dental Corps The 1st and 2nd class orderlies wore

Royal Arms. Metal helmet plate of Royal Engineers worn up to 1901

Royal Crest. Valise badge of Royal Marines, late Victorian

on their sleeves emerald green tubular braid (two bars for the 1st class, and one bar for the 2nd class).

Royal Army Medical Corps Besides the full dress of the RAMC the service dress was distinguished by the Geneva Cross arm badge (q.v.) before the First World War. Later the 1st and 2nd class orderlies had cherry-coloured tubular braid on the lower sleeves, two rows for the 1st and one for the 2nd class. In 1968 the badge of a rod and serpent was authorised for those qualified in First Aid.

Royal Crest The Lion of England standing on the Imperial Crown is the royal crest and appears on many badges.

Royal blue The facings of royal regiments (if they wear a red coat) are a deep blue, almost blue-black at times. The scarlet and blue dress was the king's livery in the 17th century. The blue was at first very light, almost sky blue as this was ordered by James I in 1622 for the ribbon of the Order of the Garter. With the advent of the House of Hanover, dark blue was taken into wear thus distinguishing Hanoverian troops from those of the Pretender who still wore red coats with light blue in the French Army.

Royal colours Red and blue were the livery colours of the Stuarts. Henry VIII had a royal standard of these colours and Charles I dressed his Guards in red and blue. At the Restoration Charles II not only dressed his Foot Guards in these colours but also other troops including artillery. In the 18th century the drummers' lace of royal regiments was yellow and blue according to a warrant of 1768. In the 19th century the colours of trumpet and bugle cords for royal regiments were red, yellow and blue which remained in use into the present century.

Royal regiments Regiments which were commanded by the king were obviously royal regiments. Those which were named after the queen or princes of royal blood did not, at first, have the royal blue facings, although they did later. In modern times many corps are named royal, especially services, but they do not have what are considered royal colours.

Royal Stuart tartan As the sovereign belongs to the Stuart (Stewart) clan certain regiments have the privilege of wearing the Royal Stuart tartan, the pipers of the Scots Guards (who have the sovereign as colonel-in-chief) being one. The Royal Scots who wore the Hunting Stuart tartan for trews were granted the Royal Stuart for pipers on the 300th Anniversary of naming of the regiment by King George V. Pipers of the King's Own Scottish Borderers, the Black Watch and once the 9th Battalion of the Highland Light Infantry were also allowed this tartan.

Royal Warrant In the case of uniforms the Royal Warrants of 1751 and 1768 were very important for they gave instructions as to the regulation of uniform in the British regular army.

RS These initials within laurel sprays appear to refer to regimental scouts in the last part of the First World War.

Rubberised clothing Known as early as the Crimean War this had an erratic existence. See 'water-proofing' and 'groundsheets'.

Runner This is a loose band of metal on shoulder-belts which can be moved to keep the free end of a belt in place. On headdress straps and other cords the runner is a piece of material by which two straps may be made tight as they slide together. Also on the busby line around the neck.

Russia braid A narrow braid of double weave, often gold wire on thread measuring from one-eighth of an inch up to one-quarter of an inch. Suitable for ornamenting tunics and jackets. Black and other colours may be used for rifle regiments.

Russian leather A durable leather treated with birch-bark oil. Used for swordbelts of British general officers and certain other officers in the 19th century.

Russia braid. On pocket of Royal Artillery mess waistcoat

113

S The letter 's' signifies the Surveyor, RA, introduced in 1923, within a thicker laurel wreath than on other trade badges. The 1st class surveyor had the addition of a crown but the battery surveyor when introduced had a simple 's'. The 's' and wreath only is worn today.

S and rifles It is said that the 's' in a wreath was worn by the sniper in the First World War but during the Second World War an 's' over crossed rifles in a wreath was worn. Later it was changed to the 's' over crossed rifles which were close together at the top.

Säbelkoppel German, sword strap.

Säbeltasche German, sabretache.

Sabretache Derived from the German, a pocket or pouch (tasche) attached to a sabre (sword). The early Hungarian hussars wore tight breeches which did not permit pockets and so their purse or pouch (like the mediaeval *giperne*) was worn on a waist-belt. Although worn extensively on the Continent sabretaches were not introduced to British cavalry until the end of the 18th century. Light dragoons and hussars took them into wear and in 1812 heavy cavalry also had them. Troopers of heavy cavalry discontinued wearing sabretaches in 1831 but they were not completely abolished until 1902.

Sack coat A dark blue flannel coat worn for fatigue purposes in the American Civil War was named a sack coat in paragraph 1457 of the 1861 regulations.

Saddler The trade of saddler in the British Army did not have the badge of a saddle (as in some other armies) but that of the bit (q.v.) also worn by the collar-makers.

Saddle-tree-maker Also wears the trade badge of a bit.

Safa, safah Indian cavalry headdress made of long piece of cloth.

Saloo Muslin cloth used in India.

Sam Browne belt A special sword-belt designed by General Sir Sam Browne who lost his left arm and could not easily draw his sword from the scabbard. By converting some of his horse harness he suspended the sword on short straps, had a shoulder-strap go over the right shoulder and for good measure created a place for a pistol holster on the waist-belt. His practical design spread all over the world.

Sandals In hot climates such as China and Africa, sandals were worn by the native soldiery but their European officers and NCOs wore boots or shoes.

Sashes Originally a necessity to show national colours before the evolution of uniform, the sash (or scarf) was worn both over the shoulder and around the waist, usually the former by infantry and the latter by cavalry. British officers wore a red or crimson silk

Sabretache. Officer, Royal Gloucester Hussars

Saddler. Embroidered arm badge of horse's bit

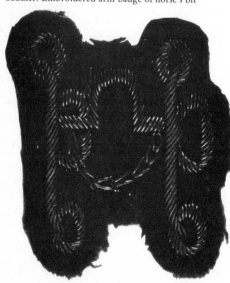

sash. By the middle of the 18th century British sergeants had the red sash with a central stripe of the facing colour (or other colours) but in 1845 the coloured stripe was discontinued. Although the officer's silk sash in the 18th century was wide and strong enough to be used as a sling or hammock, the common waist pattern introduced under AO40 of 1902 was a folded and sewn item with attached hanging ends. The Highland Officer's sash remained over the left shoulder in the old tradition but with a sewn knot on the right hip. The sergeant's sash is worn over the right shoulder. While the majority of sashes are in the National colour, there are colours like the black of the RTR and the blue of the Royal Corps of Signals.

St Edward's Crown The Tudor or Imperial crown (q.v.) was replaced in 1953 by the St Edward's crown which was to be borne by the troops of Her Majesty Queen Elizabeth II on badges, buttons and elsewhere.

Saw-edge A distinctive embroidery pattern used for loops on coats of ADCs and equerries in the 19th century.

SB These embroidered initials as an arm badge indicate British Army stretcher-bearer in the first part of the 20th century.

Scabbard The sheath to a sword, bayonet or pointed weapon.

Scales (a) Chin scales are overlapping pieces of metal, sewn on to the chinstrap of a helmet or other headdress; (b) shoulder-scales are also overlapping pieces of metal, sometimes loose in the case of wings and epaulettes of the early 19th century, or fixed into a rigid shape as worn later upon undress jackets of cavalrymen or bandsmen.

Scarf (a) Worn by drum-majors of Foot Guards around the waist in State clothing; (b) tartan scarves are worn by pipers, drummers and bandsmen in some Highland regiments; (c) the Queen's Scarf of Boer War vintage was thought to have been an award and even of rank, was intended for gallant soldiers but without any additional military award and only as a welfare gift.

Scarlet This colour has been a distinguishing feature of the English from the 16th century and the royal soldiers of Charles II's reign all wore red coats, even the artillerymen. See also 'Royal Colours'.

Schabracke German, the horse cloth which went under the saddle. These items were usually embroidered in the corners with regimental or rank devices. In the British army cavalry officers discontinued shabraques at the end of Queen Victoria's reign.

Schabrunke German, the holster cap which went in front of the saddle.

Schachel-hue Danish, the shaped felt cap worn by hussars. See also 'mirliton'.

Schako, tschako See shako.

Schapska Polish, lance cap.

Schwarawarder See charivara.

Scharfe German, scarf.

Scheide German, scabbard.

Schirm German, peak or shade to a headdress.

Schirm-mütze German, peaked cap.

Schnüre German, lace or cord.

Schulterklappe German, shoulder-strap.

Schulter stücke German, ornament on the shoulder.

Schuppenketten German, metal scale strap.

Schwalbennesten German, swallow's nest (q.v.).

Scottish dress The national dress of Scotland (including tartan) was worn by the Black Watch without interruption from their beginnings up to the present day. The items of Highland dress may be referred to under bonnet, breccan, doublet, feather bonnet, hose, plaid, garter flashes, moggan, etc.

Scout The trained scout of a cavalry regiment in the early 20th century had a special arm badge, that of a fleur-de-lys, the accepted

Scottish dress. Officers of Black Watch, c.1846

Scout. Embroidered arm badge of trained scouts

symbol for the north on a compass or a map. Worn on the right arm above the elbow the highest qualification had the addition of a cross below. Made in both metal and embroidery these signs disappeared after the First World War.

Sealed pattern When a band of officers (or other responsible persons) approved the quality and finish of an item of clothing, it was sealed with the wax of the Board of Ordnance or other government seal to be recognised as the standard to be kept by manufacturers. There was valuable evidence to be seen on these patterns because they also carried the date of approval and obsolescence. Such details are not always to be found today.

Sealskin cap Sealskin was worn in Canada for winter caps and mitts. The Kings Royal Rifle Corps and the Rifle Brigade wore shakos up to 1873 when the riflemen took sealskin caps. These lapsed when the helmet was introduced but came back into wear in July 1890, the Royal Irish Rifles also adopting the fur cap, soon after.

Secrete Cavalrymen wore an iron skull cap or protection under the hat as a safeguard against sword-cuts in the eighteenth century after the iron helmet went out of fashion.

Seitengewehr German, for side arm.

Serge A thick cloth with a diagonal weave popular for uniform including undress serge jackets.

Sergeant, serjeant This NCO in the 17th century was distinguished in the British Army by the halbert (q.v.) which he carried. By the end of the century lace was added to the coat seams, silver lace sometimes being used. Sashes were also worn. In the 18th century rank distinctions were known to have appeared on the shoulders but chevrons only appeared at the turn of the century to indicate grades (q.v. sashes, chevrons).

Sergeant-major In 1761 it was ordered that only the sergeant-major and the drum-major would wear silver lace. This metal was worn on the collar and on the epaulette fringe. When chevrons were regularised in 1802 four were worn above the elbow by sergeants-major. Changes of status and groupings as staff-sergeants brought about other rank distinctions including a crown and crown and wreath, etc.

Serpent (and/or rod) The use of snake venom in Ancient Greece for medical purposes led to the use of the serpent as a badge for medical officers and personnel throughout Europe and America. (See also rod and serpent.)

Service dress Obviously a dress for service conditions rather than full or ceremonial dress. The general introduction of khaki or service drab in the British Army in 1902 is detailed in the 1904 Dress Regulations.

Service stripes (a) Good conduct (and long service) badges had been introduced in the last year of William IV's reign. They had been worn on the right arm above the cuff point upwards but in 1881 they were transferred to the left arm still point upwards (with

Shako. Officers, 37th Foot, pattern of 1861–9

Shell jacket. Officer, 49th Foot, c.1840

the exception of the drummers of the Foot Guards who wore them point downward so as not to be confused with the ornamental darts on the sleeves); (b) war service stripes were introduced in the First World War (1918–22) and again in the Second World War (1944–5) with a chevron to indicate each year of service.

Sgian dhu, skean dhu Gaelic, 'black knife'. Worn in the top of the right hose by Highlanders from c.1830. Considered a civilian item then but now worn in full Highland dress by officers and other soldiers.

Shabraque The cloth or skin worn on a horse derived from the Turkish *tashprak* – saddledeck.

Shag A long-napped rough cloth popular for breeches and vests of British heavy cavalry in the 18th century.

Shagreen Rough grained leather usually dyed green; used for sword-scabbards.

Shako From *czak*, Magyar for peak. A peaked cap. Issued under General Order of 23 February 1800 to British infantry; this pattern known as the 'stovepipe'). The high flat-topped cap had been worn by the Austrian infantry in the 18th century. Worn in a number of shapes by the British infantry (as well as some cavalry and artillery) until the introduction of the helmet c.1878. The British types ranged from the stovepipe, through the Belgic or Waterloo cap to the Regency, Bell-topped, Albert French and Quilted. May be spelt in a variety of ways – chaco, schako, tschako etc. but for the purpose of clarity 'shako' is used here for the British Army.

Shalloon A lining cloth made at Chalon, France.

Shamrock lace A metal lace or braid woven with the pattern of shamrocks to be worn by Irish regiments as in the 8th Royal Irish Hussars and the 4th Dragoon Guards.

Shawl No one would dream of calling the Highland shoulder plaid a shawl but this term has been applied to the item worn by Irish pipers. In the Irish Guards green cloaks are worn but for others like the Ulster Defence Regiment they have a shawl of piper-green lined with scarlet.

Sheepskin (or lambskin) These were used in horse-furniture at the beginning of the 19th century for light cavalry. Black sheepskin instead of white was recommended in 1833 for lancers. Later the new 19th, 20th and 21st regiments of light cavalry had sheepskins but no shabraques. Whereas officers of the Life Guards preferred black bearskins the Royal Horse Guards had black lambskins for their undress shabraques. Black sheepskins without facings were adopted for all ranks of the Royal Horse Guards for their undress shabraques.

Shell jacket This garment, reminiscent of an Eton College jacket was officially introduced to rank and file of British infantry in 1830. This red jacket replaced the white waistcoat as a fatigue dress and lasted until about 1872 when it was replaced by the kersey frock. The white shell or the white drill jacket (q.v.) continued in wear by Highlanders and Foot Guards (also see fatigue jacket). Infantry officers changed the undress coat for the shell jacket about the same time as other ranks and kept it until 1856 when the frock coat was substituted for duties. The shell jacket continued for mess dress but eventually evolved into a new pattern.

Shirt In the 18th century the soldiers' shirts were white cotton or linen. Ordinary patterns were called ammunition shirts for the men. There were also 'bosomed' shirts. In Victorian times the 'greyback' shirt was well known. The khaki shirt introduced with the service dress of khaki was collarless until a crude addition was made at the end of the Second World War.

Shoes Infantrymen's shoes followed the civilian patterns. In the 17th century they were tanned leather with ribbon bows. In the last quarter of the 17th century ornamental shoe buckles were fastened on the instep. In the 18th century the square-toed front was still in use. By the reign of George 1 bows were replaced by shoe strings or cords, but buckles continued in use for the military man. Ankle boots for infantry were introduced in 1822 and the use of shoes (except in Highland regiments) was discontinued.

Shoeing smith The badge for this military trade is the horse shoe (q.v. also farrier).

Shorts The idea of shortened trousers appears to have begun in Africa for the Askaris in Kumassi in 1873 wore them. Elsewhere in Africa they began to be worn and by 1904 khaki shorts were worn in India. Apart from the tropical point of view they were worn for health reasons in Europe during the First World War when khaki trousers were cut down. A change in medical opinion led to 'shorts, khaki drill' being declared obsolete.

Shoulder-belt Belts worn over the shoulder include those needed to carry a pouch, a carbine, a sword or a bayonet – or even those now worn for ornamental reasons by cavalry and rifle officers where the pouch originally was intended to carry ammunition (q.v. pouches, etc.).

Shoulder-chains There was a short period when yeomanry regiments wore wings or straps of chain in the early 19th century but the main revival was in India after the Mutiny. By the end of the 19th century, British cavalry regiments and Royal Horse Artillery were wearing shoulder-chains on service dress. Today many cavalry and yeomanry units wear the chains on their blue tunics.

Shoulder-cords In 1880 the badges of rank for officers were moved from the collar to the shoulders. In full dress gold or silver cord was worn as a kind of shoulder strap and the embroidered badges were placed at the shoulder ends. In the modern ceremonial dress gold cords with coloured backings are mainly worn but silver cords denote the Special Air Service, Light Infantry and black in the case of rifle regiments.

Shoulder-knot These were worn on the right shoulder in the first half of the 18th century slightly down the back to keep the

Shoulder-chains. Metal rank and/or regimental markings may be added.

Shoulder-scale. 14th King's Light Dragoons, *c.*1840

sword belt from slipping off the shoulder. It is depicted in the 1742 'Cloathing Book'. It later developed into a rank distinction and led the way to the epaulette.

Shoulder-plaid When the belted plaid was divided into two, the lower part became the kilt and the upper part was fastened at the shoulder and also worn around the body over the left shoulder. See also plaid, scarf.

Shoulder-scales These ornaments of over-lapping pieces of metal were worn by British cavalrymen officially from 1843. Officers wore them for undress clothing by 1843. Troopers discontinued shoulder-scales in the Crimean War but certain yeomanry regiments wore them for many years later.

Shoulder-straps To keep belts from slipping off the shoulder, ribbon and knots were used. It was not until the 18th century was well under way that the idea of a shoulder-strap with a button was considered. Even then many years passed before the common soldier was given two straps. In 1907, the colour of the strap changed from that of the tunic to that of the facing colour. Embroidered regimental titles (or metal) were added to denote the unit.

Shoulder-title The introduction of service drab dress in 1902 saw the official use of the shoulder-title normally in a curved shape about one inch below the shoulder seam. Distinctive colours were chosen for the various arms of the service. Although replaced temporarily by the metal title on the strap the cloth titles or initials returned and were worn on the battle-dress. The pieces of cloth known as 'slip-ons' were intended to be removed in action.

Side arms These are the personal weapons worn at the side of a soldier like a sword, bayonet or pistol.

Signal flag The arm badge of crossed signal flags (in blue and white) awarded to skilled visual signallers was authorised in 1866 and is still worn today.

Silk This now expensive material was used for officers' coat linings in early days but was not a hard-wearing material. It is still employed in the crimson scarves of the drum-majors of the Foot Guards and for such embroidered examples as trumpet and drum banners, as well as standards, guidons and regimental colours.

Silver A metal used for officers' buttons, breastplates and other parts of uniform. Until 1830 a regular regiment could have had either silver or gold distinctions but after that date gold was restricted to the regulars and silver was to denote the militia or volunteers. In 1881 the militia battalions became linked with the regular regiments and thus took gold, volunteer battalions receiving the same distinction in 1908. Today silver is a distinction of Light Infantry and the Special Air Services.

Silver Stick A distinction for certain officers closely connected with the sovereign. See Gold Stick for details.

Ski-cap Although a Scandinavian headdress, the shape had

Shoulder-title. Royal Artillery, scarlet on dark blue

proved very suitable for military use. The Austrians wore it in the First World War, followed by the Swiss and German troops. British and American troops have taken it into wear since the Second World War.

Skill-at-arms To encourage the soldier to be proficient, prize badges were awarded for his skill in musketry, swordsmanship, and gunnery, for which he was awarded a prize, and wore an appropriate arm badge. Later these awards were named as skill-at-arms and extended to cover the use of other weapons as well as skill in driving, distance-judging and other aspects. See under separate headings for the badges to be worn on the arm.

Skirt The lower portions of a coat or jacket may be known as the skirt or skirts. Worn loose in the early 18th century the skirts were later turned back temporarily to aid marching and then permanently sewn back. With the split down the back there were four portions to be turned back and fastened with hook and eye. When eventually these skirts were sewn down the places where originally fastened became elaborated into embroidered skirt-ornaments which usually bore the regimental number and device.

Skull-cap A metal cap was worn under the hat as protection against sword blows in the 18th century. See also calotte, secrète.

Skull and cross-bones These gruesome objects seem to date back to the Thirty Years War where a favourite symbol for banners was a skull and a laurel wreath, indicating 'death or glory'. Thus when raised the 17th Light Dragoons (later 17th Lancers) chose the badge of a skull and cross-bones with the words 'or glory' to be placed on their appointments.

Slide A moving loop of metal to keep the loose end of a buckled strap in position.

Slings These are the straps from which may be slung a sword, a sabretache or a musket. They may be plain leather or ornamented with gold or silver embroidery.

Slouch hat No doubt the broad-brimmed colonial hat worn by the Australians in Queen Victoria's reign led to its adoption in the South African War. With the brim turned up at the side, it could carry a badge or a device to indicate the unit. The British Army adopted it in 1902 not only for wear abroad but at home. It lapsed in Britain although it continued in colonial service. It was popular with at least one Scottish yeomanry regiment but made a comeback in the Second World War as a bush hat to be worn in the Far East as well as parts of Africa.

Smasher A nickname for the slouch hat.

Smith A blacksmith had the trade badge of a horseshoe, a symbol in use as early as the 18th century.

Snake-hook The 's'-shaped hook to a waist-belt was used in the early 19th century, popular as an undress item but also worn by riflemen.

Snow-shoes These large racquet-shaped objects of wood and sinew are worn with moccasins in America to traverse the snow

Skull and cross-bones. Metal badge of 17th (later 17/21st) Lancers

Sphinx. Metal badge, worn by several regiments.

Sporran. Officer's pattern, 79th Camerons and 92nd Highlanders

as the wide area which they cover serves to prevent the wearer sinking into the snow.

Solar, sola helmet Sola, from the Hindi, is the pith from which sun helmets were made. Such helmets also offered protection for the solar (sun's) rays.

Sommerrocke German, a summer coat or tunic of white material.

Sonderheit-abzeichen German, distinctions for specialists.

Soubrevest, supervest, supraveste An overgarment worn by Gardes de Corps. See also *supervest* or special bodyguards, wearing this clothing.

Sowar Indian horseman or trooper.

SP These initials with laurels on an arm badge denote special proficiency *c.* 1939–50.

Spats, spatterdashes Gaiters to protect the legs from mud and spatters.

Sphinx The campaign in Egypt brought the award, for British troops, in 1801 of the 'Sphinx and Egypt' which was to be borne on the appointments of men who actually took part. Later it was widened to cover regiments who were present and is to be seen on many regimental badges and colours.

Spine pad Spine pads to protect the backbone from excessive heat were worn about 1908 in Sierra Leone. In 1910 the spine pad was officially introduced but they went out of favour although still in use in India in 1942.

Spitze German, point or peak as on a bicorn hat.

Spontoon, espontoon A staved weapon carried by officers from Charles II's reign until the American War 1775–83 when it went out of fashion. The sergeant's pike of 1791–1830 is sometimes called a spontoon.

Sporran Gaelic, the purse worn in front of the kilt.

Spur The arm badge of qualified rough rider, riding instructor (q.v.).

Spur and whip (whips) The arm badge of a qualified driver (q.v.) of horses, see also whip.

Spur leathers These are the pieces of leather worn in front of boot through which went the spur straps.

Spurs Worn by mounted men at all periods in all armies. Also worn by the Royal Corps of Signals, even though they were not a mounted unit (except on motor-cycles) when formed but they were derived from a mounted corps, the Royal Engineers. Certain officers in infantry regiments (such as the field officers and adjutant) who needed horses on parade wore spurs. There are many patterns of spurs, sometimes as many as three different patterns for one regiment.

Stable belt Intended as a practical belt to keep up trousers, stable belts have developed into coloured strips with regimental and corps patterns. The coloured girdles worn before the Great War may have been the inspiration. The 'dress' girdles now worn are

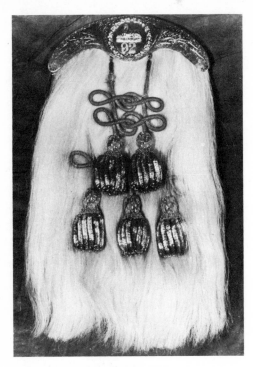

Star. Whole star and half-star worn in ACF

frequently little more than the stable belt with special metal plates in front.

Stable dress The dress worn for stable duties had to be a simplified working dress with a cap, a loose jacket and trousers, frequently of a coarse material such as canvas for the suit.

Staff The staff carried by the drum-major (also called a mace) is now a long stick with an ornamental top and chains. It is said to have developed from the cane carried for punishment from the days when drummers were expected to carry out beatings.

Stag's head The device of a stag's head is frequently found as a badge in Scottish regiments. In the case of the Earl of Seaforth it commemorates the occasion when King Alexander II of Scotland was saved by a member of the clan.

Stahl helm German, steel helmet.

Standard Besides being a flag, a standard is also the sealed pattern of clothing being the example or standard approved for manufacturers.

Star (a) Five-pointed: (i) awarded in the British Army for distance judging. Introduced at the beginning of the 20th century, the gold star was worn on the right arm below the elbow. Discontinued after the First World War, (ii) worsted star for 1st class driver Royal Tank Corps in the First World War. Adopted for all mechanical transport drivers in 1950, (iii) volunteers in late Victorian times wore a silk or worsted star to indicate five years service; (b) four-pointed: (i) sergeants in the British Army in the late 19th century wore a one-and-a-half-inch diameter star above all others in the same material as the chevron, (ii) red silk star one-and-a-half inches wide worn by cadets for Certificate 'A' (q.v.). In 1974 the new Army proficiency stars were marked by the numbers '1' and '2' on blue silk and '3' and '4' on red silk stars (see also ACF); (c) other stars were worn by quartermasters and subaltern officers (see under respective headings).

As stars represented the states in the National Flag of the United States, it is fitting that stars should also be rank badges for their general officers. The brigadier-general had one star, the major-general two and the lieutenant-general three. The full general at one time had a golden eagle between two stars but this was altered to four silver stars about the time of the First World War. The rank of General of the Army, when it was created, had five silver stars. In the Confederate Army, the major wore one star, the lieutenant-colonel two stars, the colonel three and the general had three stars within a wreath.

Star loop This was an elaborate embroidered loop worn on the cocked hats of cavalrymen in the first part of the 19th century, especially for levée dress.

Star plate The British shako of Regency and later periods as well as the helmet had a large star or ribbed plate to back the regimental devices. A similar device to make for unity of design was also worn on the belt plates and produced a most imposing effect.

Star-plate. Helmet plate of Dorsetshire Regiment, late 19th century

Steel helmet Although an iron or steel helmet may have been worn long before it was not until the First World War that a bullet-proof helmet was designed. The French Army in 1915 after trying mess-tins in the kepi, issued helmets which were not considered very effective. In the same year the British produced their version of the steel helmet which was worn in action in March 1916. The German helmet was developed at the same time and was worn at Verdun, January 1916. Although still in use the patterns of the helmets have changed many times.

Steenkirk, steinkirk, steinkerk A loosely tied cravat with the ends drawn through a buttonhole or tucked into the coat or shirt. Named after the battle of Steinkerk, fought between the Allies and France on 3 August 1692. See also neckwear, cravat, stock.

Stick Officers of Charles II's reign carried walking-sticks. The drum-major's stick developed into the long staff or mace (q.v.). See also cane.

Stickerei German, embroidery.

Stiefel German, boots.

Stock The cravat worn by the soldier evolved into the stock or roller in the 18th century. About 1786 stocks of leather were to be worn although in the West Indies black cloth was preferred. In 1845 a more pliant stock was worn although two years later it was again stiffened. The stock was finally replaced in 1862 by a small leather tab which covered the opening of the collar.

Stockings In the days of the new army of 1660 stockings were the common legwear, a second pair 'for rowling' occasionally being worn on top. The use of gaiters hid the stocking but they were still part of the full dress for infantry until the introduction of trousers generally in 1823.

Stovepipe This description was given to the plain or upright cylindrical shako worn both in Europe and in America in the 19th century.

Stö'wasser Leggings of leather from South Africa, popular for British officers in the first part of the 20th century.

Strap Many straps are and have been worn in the military; chin-straps for headdresses, shoulder-straps, strap to Sam Browne belt, etc. See under own heading.

Stripe (a) The chevrons of rank and war service (q.v.) are also known as stripes; (b) the cloth stripes or welts down the outside of trousers, overalls or breeches are also known as stripes; (c) certain broad patterns of gold or silver lace and braid are livened by central stripes of coloured silk or other material.

Stulphandeschuhe German, gauntlet.

Sturmriemen German, chin-strap for use in storm or bad weather.

Sunken top The broad top of the shakos worn from 1812 for cavalry and 1816 for infantry had a sunken leather top.

Supervest, soubrevest A loose overgarment without sleeves worn by many Body or House Guards. Perhaps inspired by the

Swan's feathers. Plume of 4th Light Dragoons, c.1840

tabard.

Surtout A few watchcoats or centry (sentry) gowns (q.v.) had been worn in Charles II's army but in 1689 surtouts or overcoats were being considered for infantry. In 1697 they were issued every second year, but they did not continue to be a permanent issue for all soldiers.

Surveyor This was an artillery qualification introduced in the First World War. The arm badge worn in 1921 for 1st class surveyors was an 's' in a wreath with a crown above. For the other grades the crown was omitted. In 1925 the battery surveyor wore the 's' only. Today only the 's' and wreath is worn.

SW These initials appear on the arm badge of the diver qualified for shallow water where they appear under a diver's helmet.

Swaggerstick The mounted soldier carried a small cane or whip under his arm when walking-out. The infantry man was permitted a cane or swaggerstick with an ornamental head. Went out of fashion after the First World War.

Swallow's nest The barred wings worn by drummers and musicians was so named in the German army. See *schwalbennester*.

Swan's feathers These beautiful feathers were worn on the headdress of General officers, Gentlemen-at-Arms, lancers and at times drum-majors of the Royal Artillery and the Royal Scots Greys.

Swedish cuff This was a simple round cuff, originally turned up and held in place with two buttons on top but later the buttons were moved to the back.

T

T and flashes. Embroidered arm badge of telecommunications technician.

T The letter 'T' with laurels was the arm badge of a British tracker in the anti-aircraft artillery during the Second World War.

T and flashes This is the arm badge for telecommunications technician.

Tab A leather tab worn in the collar opening replaced the stock in 1862.

Tabi Japanese shoes, in Second World War frequently made with the big toe separate.

Tag (or aglet) The point or metal end to a lace for a doublet or armour.

Taffeta A type of silk used for lining coats, for scarves, and for standards, guidons and colours, especially in the 17th and 18th centuries.

Talma The 1861 uniform regulation for the Army of the United States speaks of a gutta-percha talma or cloak extending to the knees with long sleeves worn by the enlisted men of cavalry.

Tam-o-shanter A Scottish bonnet made with a broad top and a tourie (or bobble) on top. In khaki the service headdress of Scottish troops. Said to be named after the poem by Robert Burns.

Tank The badge of an embroidered tank was worn by all personnel of the British Tank Corps, later the Royal Tank Regiment. This is a regimental sign rather than a trade badge and is worn on the upper right arm. It is also in the cap and collar badges.

Tape A cotton or linen material used to strengthen button-holes and also for chevrons, collars and shoulder straps. Puttees also have tapes.

Tara brooch The tara brooch is of Celtic origin and found in the tombs of the ancient Tara kings. The brooch may be seen worn by certain modern Irish pipers.

Target This British term refers to the circle of lace or braid worn on the front of the broad-topped shakos of the Regency period.

Tarleton helmet The leather helmet with a peak in front and a fur crest over the top emerged about 1780. Because it was popular with the British Legion in the American Revolution, it was named after the commander Sir Banastre Tarleton. In the official lists it was referred to as a 'cap' or a 'fur cap'. Worn by the regular light dragoons until 1812, by yeomanry for several years later and by the Royal Horse Artillery up to 1827.

Tartan Although one may know that the coloured cloth of varying patterns and stripes worn by Scotsmen is tartan, the term also applies to the plain blue or green trousers of infantry in the last part of the 19th century, as tartan is the type of weave.

Tartan hose-tops Highland hose and hose tops were originally red and white but later additional black lines and even new colours

Tarleton helmet. Officer of the 9th Light Dragoons, *c.*1800

such as red and green as in the 79th Foot appeared.

Tawny Brownish yellow or tan colour used in the scarves worn by Parliamentary troops in the English Civil War. Tawny was one of the colours in the Earl of Essex's coat-of-arms.

TE These initials in Old English characters appeared on the epaulettes and buttons of the Corps of Topographical Engineers, who were formed from the American Corps of Engineers in 1838. The Topographical Engineers were disbanded in 1863.

Technician British qualified soldier-tradesmen may wear an arm badge signifying their own speciality such as radar, telecommunications and equipment where the initials and electric flashes form the badge.

Telescope Although carried by some officers in the 17th and 18th centuries there was no official case to be worn on the person as there was for the field glasses or binoculars. Officers in the Peninsular campaigns are known to have purchased their own cases.

Tenor drums The drummers who carry these large side-drums in modern times often have tiger (and other animal) skins as aprons to match that worn by the bass-drummer. There is no special badge for the tenor-drummer.

Tent-hat This nickname is given to a folding undress cap which may have been inspired by the French and Belgian pattern. Worn by yeomanry in Victorian times and since the Second World War by the 8th King's Royal Irish Hussars and the 10th Hussars.

Tenue French, for dress – *tenue de campaigne* (service dress), *tenue de ville* or *sortie* (walking-out) and *grand tenue* (full dress).

Terai hat Although illustrated in the 1900 Dress Regulations the extent of its use is not known as nothing appears in the text. This hat turned up on the right and had a plaited pugri.

Thistle lace Gold (or silver) lace (q.v.) with the pattern of thistles was worn by Scottish regiments in full dress.

Thistle star The Star of the Order of the Thistle has been worn by Scottish regiments as a headdress badge, also on belt-plates and elsewhere.

Throat plume The long hair plume hanging from the bridle of some horses.

Thistle lace. Infantry officers and also of Scots Greys

Tiger. Badge of Leicestershire Regiment showing
Indian tiger.

Throat crescent The metal badge of a crescent was worn by
light cavalry from a throat strap and besides being decorative it
was the place to attach a picketing rope or chain.

Tie When officers in the British Army wore open-necked tunics
before the First World War in Africa and elsewhere, a shirt and
tie was part of the dress. Ties were not issued to other ranks until
the latter part of the Second World War when the battledress
blouse was permitted to be worn open. Bow ties have long been
worn with mess dress.

Tiger Worn as a cap badge by the regiments granted the 'Royal
Tiger' for service in India by the 17th Royal Leicestershire, 65th
York and Lancashire and the 67th Royal Hampshire regiments of
foot and as a collar badge by the Gordon Highlanders.

Tigerskin As these animals were shot by officers serving in India
they were put to regimental use and besides decorating the mess
rooms were worn as aprons by bass-drummers and later by tenor-
drummers.

Tin hat Colloquial expression for steel helmet (q.v.).

Tjerkeska The long cossack gown which had cartridge loops on
either side of the chest.

TM The arm badge for men of the British Army during the
First World War operating the trench mortar had these initials
combined with laurel sprays.

Tombstone hat This term was applied to the American headdress which had a false front like the British 'Waterloo' shako.

Topee Another name for solar helmet (q.v.).

Top hat A variety of top hat was worn by soldiers and marines
at the end of the 18th century for service abroad in Flanders and
Egypt. At home top hats with extra trimmings made military
helmets reminiscent of the Tarleton helmet for volunteer infantry.
The top hat went out of military use early in the next century.

Tornister German, pouch or haversac.

Tourie, toorie The short ends (or bobble) on top of a Scottish
bonnet (either glengarry or kilmarnock).

Trabant The men of the 'Trabanter' guard were ceremonial
house troops attached to some European courts. The German word
means 'satellite', a kind of henchman.

Tracing This cord or braid which usually made an ornamental
pattern around a thick cord or braid, formed 'eyes', 'trees',
'feathers', and similar designs.

Tradesmen As men fighting with weapons needed those skilled
in conservation, preparation and other non-destructive services,
there were many specially paid groups. The farrier, smith, saddler,
wheeler, cook, clerk and other trades frequently displayed their
own arm badge (q.v. under separate heading). To reduce the
number of trades, groupings under headings of 'A', 'B', 'C' and 'D'
were made in the British Army in 1958 although these were later
reduced to 'A' and 'B' only.

Trained soldier When young guardsmen qualified as trained

Trained soldier. Embroidered arm badge for young guardsmen

soldiers, they are permitted to wear a special arm badge. This embroidered device has the words 'TRAINED SOLDIER' below a 'Guards' star.

Trench mortar Men skilled with this weapon in the First World War wore on their upper arm an embroidered blue grenade. After the war the letters 'TM' were used as an arm badge (q.v. grenade and 'TM').

Tresse German, lace or braid.

Trews Scottish for trousers.

Tricorn, tricorne A three-cornered hat (q.v. hat).

Tricolor French, for three colours referring to the blue, white and red of the French National flag, also the cockade as evolved in Revolutionary days.

Troddel German, infantry sword-knot.

Tropical dress A lightweight grey uniform was worn in Tangiers when the English were present in the days of Charles II but little attempt was made to produce a tropical dress until the end of the 18th century. In the West Indies jackets and loose trousers replaced the red coat and breeches. In India white covers to headdresses and white hats were worn before 1800 but it needed the strenuous conditions of the Indian Mutiny to introduce the lightweight khaki dress which became 'universal' at the end of the 19th century. White clothing although suitable for peacetime changed to the strong but lightweight jungle green of the post Second World War period. Modern medical thought has abolished the sun helmet, the spine pad and the shorts as unnecessary.

Trousers, trowsers Loose nether garments reaching to the ankles. Originally for drill and fatigue purposes but introduced for fighting in the early 19th century and eventually became common wear in 1827.

Trumpet The badge of a trumpet was worn by the Mounted Rifles of the United States (q.v.) from 1850 to 1861.

Trumpeter The mounted trumpeter of modern times wears an arm badge of crossed trumpets (not a single trumpet as some other nations). In the 18th century the trumpeter wore a coat of reversed facings (q.v.) but in the next century wore the same garment as the trooper but differentiated by the lace.

Tsarouchia Greek, the evzone's shoes.

Tschako German for shako.

Tschapska German, for lance cap.

Tuch German, cloth.

Tuchhose German, cloth trousers.

Tudor The heraldically approved crown of 1900/1 (commonly called the King's crown) was the Imperial crown with the curved hoops, nine pearls on each side arm and five down the front or central bar.

Tuft (a) The woollen ball or shape in the front of the shako was called a tuft; (b) the fringe on the shoulders at the end of battalion company shoulder-straps was called a tuft; (c) the two rosettes of

Tunic. Full dress, other ranks', 109th Foot, c.1900

ribbons on the gorget (q.v.) were also known as tufts.

Tunic The coatee or coat with tails, worn by British troops up to the Crimean War, gave place in 1855 to a coat with skirts all the way round, known as a tunic, which thus gave protection to the stomach. The British had been slow to adopt the tunic which had been worn many years before by the French and German troops.

Turbans Although an Eastern headdress, Turkish or Moorish turbans were worn by coloured musicians in the British Army in the early part of the 18th century. The light dragoons had a small but stout headdress with a piece of cloth around it which was intended to fall down to protect the neck. This later became fixed with small chains and was known as the turban until the Tarleton helmet went out of fashion. In the Indian Army the turban was worn by native troops. There were many patterns ranging from the one on a rigid metal frame to the loosely tied type. British officers created regimental patterns which could be worn over a kullah or a pag depending on the religion or race of the wearer.

Turnback The front of the soldier's coat when folded back might be considered as turnbacks but it was the loose skirts which fold back to form two pairs of 'tails' on the coatee that are best known as turnbacks.

Tweed This material was popular in the mid-19th century for infantry trousers.

Undress. Officer of Royal Scots Grey, *c.*1880

Uberhose German, overalls as trousers.

Uberrock German, overcoat, frock coat.

Ulan German, lancer – taken from the Tartar word *oghlana* meaning a young nobleman.

Ulanka German, the tunic worn by lancers having a plastron and the back seams piped.

Umhang German, an officer's cloak or cape.

Undergarment The garments worn under the coat in the 18th century – the waistcoat, and breeches being referred to as under-garments.

Under-officer A rank given to officer-cadets in the British Army who had their own grades of seniority.

Undress The clothing of a lesser degree than (full) dress, worn for fatigues and informal occasions.

Undress cap Usually a soft cap worn with undress, although a 'pill-box' or a forage cap might be stiff, yet comfortable.

Uniform Strictly speaking uniform should be a dress with 'uniform' or exactly similar details for each man throughout the unit. Actually uniform has many rules to cover variations between ranks, regiments or corps and even between battalions. The authorities' task is to create as near as possible a 'universal' uniform (as in the Canadian armed forces) but units must have and strive to create their own personal distinctions.

Union flag This is the flag combining the Crosses of the Saints of England, Scotland and Wales. The 'Union Jack' is a naval term, not military. Thus the first colour in an infantry regiment is the 'Union'.

Unterkamisol German, a type of sleeved waistcoat worn by infantry. It was usually grey in colour but in 1817 the German regiments adopted white.

Valise The infantry soldier's pack of the late 18th century. The knapsack equipment was considered unsatisfactory and after extensive trials begun in 1865 a new valise equipment was finally approved and worn in 1871. Originally the valise was worn on the hips but by 1882 was raised to the centre of the back. The valise was also a cavalry container, not for the man but to go on the horse.

Valise ornament British Foot Guards, who had always favoured a pouch or pack ornament, each chose a distinctive brass badge to wear on the valise. The Worcestershire Regiment also wore their distinctive star plate in brass.

Vareuse French, 20th century tunic with closed and turned-down collar which carried the *pattes de collett* to distinguish units.

Velvet This material was occasionally used in military dress. The grenadier caps of the 18th century were of cloth for the men but velvet for officers. In the British Army (just after 1815) dragoon guards adopted regimental facings of velvet to distinguish themselves from the cloth of the dragoons. The State clothing of Household musicians has velvet facings. Certain corps also favour velvet facings, like the Royal Engineers who have velvet for the officers and plush for NCOs and men.

Ventilator This covers a small hole, usually gauze-covered on the shako where the outside metal-piece is in the shape of a fanciful head or ornament. On topees and blue helmets there was also a ventilator hidden under the top projection.

Vest The garment worn under the mess jacket.

Visor American caps have visors rather than peaks.

Vivandière French, woman attached to regiment or corps to supply food and drink, usually wearing 'elements' of the unit's uniform but with feminine articles of clothing.

Voltigeur hat See 'Andrews' hat.

Volunteers The regular British Army had their uniforms supplied by the nation but volunteers were expected to find their own, thus economy and fresh ideas produced unusual uniforms. The infantry volunteers of Napoleonic times wore blue as well as red or green coats. After the Peace of Amiens blue was restricted to artillery volunteers and some yeomanry and the use of red encouraged. These volunteers disappeared at the end of the war. The new volunteers from 1860 onwards found that the civilian fabrics of grey, black or brown suited their pockets very well and allowed for local production. By 1881 many volunteer units were attached to regular regiments and they were encouraged to wear the scarlet or green. In the infantry the buttons and braid of officers were silver but the further reforms of 1908 permitted gold lace and the volunteers (except for a few exceptions) now appeared similar to the regular army.

VP These letters stood for Vulnerable Points, a branch of the Corps of Military Police which came into being in 1943. A flash of red 'VP' on a blue diamond was worn on the upper arm. This branch was disbanded at the end of the war.

Volunteers. Rifle corps of Derbyshire and Staffordshire, c.1860

Wachtmantel German, watch cloak or loose overcoat worn on guard duties or cold weather.

Waffenrock German, the tunic of 1842 was a new pattern issued to both infantry and cavalry which eventually carried regimental numbers on the shoulder-straps of infantry and numbered buttons in the cavalry.

Waistbelt The waistbelt was worn by infantrymen in the 17th century to carry the sword as well as the bayonet. By the time of the American Revolution it had become the fashion to carry it over the shoulder. In the early 19th century senior staff officers wore the waistbelt to carry the sword and other mounted officers also wore it to support the sabretache when it was introduced. Infantry officers (except Scottish) discontinued the shoulder-belt for the sword at the time of the Crimean War and had the waist-belt until the turn of the next century, when the removal of the crimson silk sash from shoulder to waist caused the suspension for the sword to go under the tunic to a web-belt. The leather and web equipment of the fighting soldier all continued to retain the waistbelt to suspend a variety of items or to connect with the straps over the shoulders.

Waistbelt clasp The clasp is a two-piece metal fastening (instead of the old one-piece plate) and infantry officers after the Crimean War had regimental patterns up to the reign of Edward VII. Cavalry regiments had a flat plate with a hidden hooking device, a pattern still in use in the army.

Waistcoat The garment worn under a coat and although shaped to the waist had flaps continuing below. In the 18th century it was issued as a fatigue or undress item, sometimes with the addition of sleeves, later to become a type of jacket. In a mess dress the under-garment is called a vest.

War service stripes In January 1918 chevrons were authorised for service overseas, one red if earned before 31 December 1914 and one blue for each year afterwards. These were worn point upwards on the lower right arm. They were discontinued in 1922 but again authorised in February 1944, to be worn singly or in groups of 2, 3, or 4 printed red on khaki.

Wasserfal German, a fringe-like ornament in the small of the back of jackets early 18th century. In gold or silver bullion for officers, yellow or white for the men.

Watchcoat Various over-garments were worn for watch duties, like the 'centry gown' (q.v.) which was worn in Charles II's reign and the great coat which became a general issue in 1811. In the 18th century however watchcoats were limited in number per regiment. The orders of the 35th Foot c.1775 speak only of one

Waistbelt clasp. Officer, Essex Regiment, c.1900

Waterloo shako. Officers pattern, *c.*1812–16

blue cloth watchcoat per company to be 'of the Hussar kind'. They were still restricted until the end of the century.

Waterbottle The use of waterbottles by soldiers is familiar as far back as Sir Philip Sydney and the wounded soldier in Queen Elizabeth's reign. The leather waterbottle was used in that and the next century. After the Restoration the stone (ironstone pottery) bottle was used by the military. In the 18th century the Germans had developed the feldflasche or tin bottle and the British took this type into use until the Napoleonic Wars. The wooden water-bottle then became popular and the drum shape continued in use until the seventies when the Italian pattern came in use. By the time of the Boer War many unofficial types were to be seen but the cloth-covered bottle became fashionable and the flattened canister shape is still to be seen in the British Army.

Waterloo shako This shako received its name from the campaign in which it became famous. It had been introduced in 1812 possibly inspired by a Portuguese type already in use. It became obsolete in 1816 and was also known as the Belgic cap, once again from the area where it was worn. The false front and weak material (pasteboard and felt) were not practical on campaigns and in bad weather. It was replaced by a broad-topped shako which had a thin top covering of leather.

Water-fall The British version of the *wasserfal* (q.v.) was worn on the jackets of light dragoons and lancers during the first half of the 18th century.

Water-proofing It is known that at the beginning of the 19th century that soldiers' greatcoats were waterproofed at the cost of two shillings and three pence a coat, but little further can be mentioned until William IV reviewed the Foot Guards in rubber-ised clothing, i.e. in waterproofed capes. In the Crimean War showerproof and rubberised clothing was worn by a number of other ranks from 1855 to 1857. As recently as 1965 attempts were made to waterproof the Household Brigade tunics.

Weapons Various weapons have been utilised as arm badges for proficiency or prize qualifications. See under lance, musket, rifle, etc.

Web-belt When infantry officers in 1901 changed to the crimson sash around the waist, the existing belt was discontinued and a lightweight web-belt was worn under the tunic. This continued to have the old pattern sword slings.

Webbing Leather equipment had been used for soldiers but towards the end of the 19th century stout webbing had been tried in the American Army and after the South African War webbing was adopted in the British Army. The bandolier equipment made by Mills appeared in 1903.

Wellington boot The boot favoured by the Duke of Wellington came to just below the knee and was worn generally in the British Army at the end of the Crimean War. It continued to be worn then as a full dress item by infantry officers. In 1951 the Foot

Wheel. Embroidered arm badge of wheeler and carpenter

Guards finally gave up the Wellington boot and replaced it with the George Boot (q.v.).

Welt A strip of cloth sewn in clothing specially on the sides of trousers, breeches and netherwear. The Life Guards have a scarlet welt between their trousers or overall stripes.

Wheel The wheel frequently appears as a trade or proficiency badge in the British Army. The embroidered wagon-wheel came into use in mid-Victorian times as a mark of the wheeler and carpenter, and later other trades. It was worn on the right arm, above chevrons in the case of a sergeant. It became obsolescent in 1950. Before the First World War a bicycle wheel appeared as the sign of proficiency. A steering wheel was introduced about 1925 as a prize badge for Drivers, i.c. It was worn only in the Royal Army Service Corps up to 1927 when the Royal Artillery also qualified. In 1939 the prize aspect disappeared but the wheel continued for skill-at-arms and all drivers could qualify. In 1950 the wheel was replaced by the badge of a star.

Whip A whip or whips combined with a spur introduced in 1877 for drivers of artillery as a prize badge but disappeared at the outbreak of the Second World War.

Whiting A chalk used as well as pipeclay to whiten soldiers' leather equipment, helmets, etc., mainly in the 19th century although continued into the next.

Whiskers In the 18th century side-whiskers might be worn by drum-majors and pioneers. Later by light cavalry and rifle officers inspired by Continental hussars. See also moustaches, beard.

Whistle Worn by officers and NCOs of rifle and light infantry regiments for field work when the employment of a bugle was not practical. Worn on the pouch-belt in an ornamental form.

White drill jackets White waistcoats had been worn in the 18th century when the coat was to be restricted to ceremonial duties. Although most infantry changed to a red waistcoat, the Foot Guards and Highland corps continued to wear the white waistcoats or jackets. In 1913 the white jackets were obsolescent but both the Foot Guards and Highlanders wore them for tattoos and tournaments after the First World War.

White Horse The 'White Horse of Hanover' came to England with the Georges. In ancient times there is a connection with the White Horse of Kent through the ancient Saxon tribes. The small frontlet on the grenadier's cloth cap had an embroidered white horse on a green mount and later it was on the cloth top of fur caps. Cavalry standards of today still have the White Horse of Hanover in the compartments. Cavalry regiments also frequently have the White Horse as a badge as do some infantry regiments.

White metal An alloy or mixture for badges and fittings of other ranks to match the silver of officers. Also used today for pipers badges and others.

Wicker helmets The sun helmets made in India c.1858 had a framework of wicker or cane with a covering of felt or cloth.

Whip. Crowned whips and spur badge for driver

Wing. With metal scales, officer, 69th Foot, *c.*1816

About ten years later the cork (or pith) helmet was adopted as a lighter and more comfortable headdress.

Wig Following the civilian practices of the 17th and early 18th centuries officers wore wigs in the latest fashion. Natural hair was worn by the men although examples of wigs for other ranks are known when the men were bald.

Wings When a shell jacket had to go over a sleeved waistcoat small pieces of cloth were added to the shoulders to hide the joints. Grenadiers and light infantry of the 18th century had these wings and continued to wear them up to the Crimean War when they were discontinued. Bandsmen and musicians who also wore wings continue to wear them to the present day. The bars on the drummer's wings were originally in the regimental braid or lace (q.v.) but today the Foot Guards continue to wear their distinctive fleur-de-lys lace. Occasionally the lace with the repeating red crown may be seen for drummers of the line. About 1822 officers of the American Light Artillery wore wings instead of epaulettes. Infantry wore silver wings but line officers of artillery and rifles had gold wings. They were discontinued in the new uniform of 1835.

Winter clothing The British Army took its time to recognise the need for a tropical or a cold-weather dress. In America blanket coats and fur caps were worn with leggings and moccasins. From the American Revolution onwards these items continued as necessary. High boots and mitts were also part of the dress in Canada. The cold weather of the Crimean campaign and the First World War saw improved clothing in use for Europe including woollen items like caps, scarves and balaclava helmets as well as fur garments. White camouflage suits and helmet covers were worn for fighting in the snow in the Second World War. The war in Korea brought much more sophisticated garments into use with padding and close-weave gaberdine, nylon and artificial fabrics now being used.

Wolseley helmet A khaki sun helmet was sealed (q.v. sealed pattern) in September 1899 and was referred to in the 1900 Dress Regulations as the Wolseley pattern cork helmet. It was worn by the West Africa and the Chinese Regiments. By the 1904 Dress Regulations it was for service at all stations abroad. A little later it was also to be of white drill and the 1911 Dress Regulations quote that plumes were to be added for General and Staff officers. By 1934 many 'embellishments' had been permitted, including feathers for the Brigade of Guards, the Royal Fusiliers, the Black Watch, the DCLI, and the Lancashire Fusiliers, with the Royal Irish Fusiliers coming in later. In January 1939 the pith helmet was authorised in India and Burma. In 1948 the tropical helmet worn in the MEF and elsewhere was abolished. See topee, etc.

Wound stripe These dress distinctions were introduced in August 1916 to indicate wounds gained on service. One gold stripe of narrow braid one-and-a-half inches long was worn upright on

Wreath. Of oak and laurel leaves on other ranks' shako plate. 3rd Foot, c.1850

the left arm to indicate each wound. Wounds for previous wars were to be marked by red rayon braid. These became obsolete in 1922 but the idea was restored in February 1944, once again becoming obsolete after the war.

Wreath A wreath is frequently used in badges, being linked with the laurel crown of Roman and earlier victories. The laurel wreath (or sprays) is included in many trade badges (q.v.) Oakleaf wreaths are also incorporated into badges thus making a connection with the Boscobel Oak of Charles II's escape and with the Hanoverians. In some cases the wreaths are of two different sprays, like oakleaves and palm. The Union wreath (q.v.) is composed of the three national flowers, roses, thistles and shamrock.

Wrist-strap In tropical dress when short sleeves (or rolled sleeves) are worn, senior NCOs who normally wear rank badges on the lower sleeve are permitted to wear a wrist-strap of cloth (or leather) on which to carry the brass rank badge.

Wülste, achelwülste German, a pad or roll as on the shoulder of infantry (including riflemen) serving to keep a belt in place.

Yeoman crown cap The American shako or cap of 1813 followed the European example and had a top wider than the base. Called a yeoman crown cap it was replaced by the bell crown cap (q.v.).

Yeomanry Being volunteer cavalry and finding their own uniforms, a great variation of dress was worn from the late 18th century onwards. Combinations of regular cavalry uniforms and frequent use of obsolete headdress produced results which cannot be covered in these short descriptions. Modern uniform often has the shoulder-chains for ceremonial dress.

Zouave dress The French Army in the East adopted zouave dress and later in the American Civil War both sides had volunteers in zouave dress. Duryea's Zouaves had the addition of a white turban around the fez while Meagers' and Wallace's Zouaves wore kepis (as did most zouave officers).

Zouave jacket The short sleeveless jacket made popular by the French zouave from North Africa became a feature of the West India Regiment after Queen Victoria's request. West Indian military units continued to wear it as later did African military (and police) formations, although in a simplified style.

Zwaluwnesten Netherlands, swallow nests, or drummer's wings.

Zouave Jacket. Worn by Hausa

Bibliography

Bibliography and sources also useful for further research.

Official Books and Documents
Dress Regulations for Officers, also for Officers of Royal Artillery and of
    Royal Engineers.
Regulations and Orders for the Army.
Rules relating to Dress.
Army Council Instructions and Army Circulars.
Clothing Regulations.
War Office papers in the Public Records Office.
Vocabularies of Clothing and Necessaries.
Catalogues of Clothing and Necessaries.
Army Equipment (seven books, 1864–6).

Periodicals
Journal of the Society for Army Historical Research.
Bulletin of the Military Historical Society.
Journal of the Royal Artillery Institution and the 'Gunner'.
'Soldier' Magazine.
Various regimental journals and military publications.
Current newspapers and illustrated publications.
Journal of the Company of Military Collectors and Historians.
National Geographical Magazine of America.

Books
Knötel, H., *Handbuch der Uniformkunde.*
Martin, P., *Military Costume.*
Walton, Clifford, *History of the Standing Army, 1660–1700.*
Dunbar, T., *History of Scottish Dress.*
Pietsch, P., *Formations – und Uniformierungsgeschichte.*
Strachan, H., *British Military Uniforms, 1768–1796.*
Kannik, P., *Military Uniforms of the World.*
Mollo, J., *Military Fashion.*
Forbes, A., *History of the Ordnance Services.*
Campbell, D. A., *Dress of the Royal Artillery.*
Armée Française Uniformes 1937.
Dress worn at Court.
Kelly and Schwabe, *History of Costume and Armour, 1066–1800.*
George Philip's military publications, including *Ranks at a Glance.*
Gale and Polden's publications, wall-charts, etc.
Boys' Own Paper. Contemporary articles and illustrations.
Howell, E. M. and Kloster, D. E., *United States Headgear to 1854.*
Nelson, H. L. and Ogden, H. A., *Uniforms of the United States.*

Places
British Museum Library.
Public Records Office.
National Army Museum.
Army Museums Ogilby Trust.
India Office Library.
Regimental and Corps museums.